HOW TO BUY RARE BOOKS

Unique engraving found in a copy of Raoul Lefevre, *The Recuyell of the Histories of Troy*, Bruges, William Caxton, *c*.1473.

The engraving shows Caxton presenting a copy of his book to Margaret of York, sister of Edward IV of England. Noble people were frequently the patrons and inspirers of authors and thus also of printers.

CHRISTIE'S COLLECTORS GUIDES

HOW TO BUY RARE BOOKS

*A practical guide to
the antiquarian book market*

WILLIAM REES-MOGG

PHAIDON · CHRISTIE'S
OXFORD

A Note on Prices

Throughout the book, dollar or pound equivalent prices have been added to prices quoted. Where the price was achieved at auction, the equivalent has been given using the conversion rate current at the time of the sale; where the price is an estimate of approximate value, the figure has been converted at a rate of £1 = $1.25 (the rate current at the time of writing). Prices for books with an international market are now often quoted in dollars, and this can lead to sharp fluctuations in the price of certain books when quoted in sterling or other currencies.

Phaidon · Christie's Limited,
Littlegate House,
St Ebbe's Street,
Oxford OX1 1SQ

First published 1985
© Phaidon · Christie's Limited 1985
Second impression 1988

British Library Cataloguing in Publication Data

How to buy rare books.
   1. Book collecting
   I. Rees-Mogg, *Sir* William
   002'.075   Z987

ISBN 0–7148–8019–1

Typeset in Apollo by Keyspools Ltd., Bridge Street, Golborne, Lancs.

Printed in Spain by H. Fournier, S.A.-Vitoria

Contents

Preface

In 1981 the Thomson family decided to sell the London *Times*, and I decided that it was time to retire after fourteen years as editor. By one of those fortunate coincidences which are the delight of book collecting, my retirement coincided with the decision of the shareholders to sell the long-established London antiquarian bookshop of Pickering & Chatto. I had been a Pickering customer for thirty years and was in love with books, so I embraced my good fortune and bought the business.

As antiquarian booksellers will tell you, it is not enough to be a collector of forty years' standing, or an ex-editor, to make a go of antiquarian bookselling. No doubt Pickering & Chatto gave me a wonderful start. The previous chairman of Pickering's, Dudley Massey, the father of Christie's present bookman in New York, Stephen Massey (to whom I am very grateful for his helpful suggestions and for reading the manuscript), had been in his time 'the best judge of a book in London'. That was John Carter's verdict, and in proof of it Dudley had left a stock of depth and quality. Pickering & Chatto had been founded in 1820 by the celebrated William Pickering, the inventor of publishers' cloth bindings and the best judge of a book in London in his generation. Still there were plenty of things I did not know about bookselling, and if I used a newspaperman's approach, that was only natural from my training.

What do you do if you take over a newspaper? You relate to your readership and you look for the best possible staff, preferably young. The reputations of old editors are made by brilliant young journalists. If there was a flaw in antiquarian bookselling—and you cannot in London teach much to Quaritch or Maggs—it was that we did not relate to our audience, or at least that we did not do enough to offer a way into the joys of book collecting for new customers. To those who become customers, book-sellers do traditionally provide a friendly welcome, with conversation and browsing and no pressing for sales. This book is for new collectors. There will, I hope, be something in it to interest all book people, but it is designed to widen the audience, or at least to inform a wider public. It is for the general reader who does not know how to set about forming a collection. I have found in my own life that collecting books has been a consistent pleasure, and an unceasing form of self-education; half at least of my store of knowledge comes from book collecting. There is nothing particularly difficult about learning to collect books. But there is a need for an introductory guide of some real substance.

That is why the book has been written. The how is the way of all good newspapers. It does not simply contain what I know; it contains the collective knowledge of Pickering & Chatto. Christopher Edwards is an ex-Christie's man and our expert on English literature. Roger Gaskell is an ex-Quaritch man and our expert on scientific and medical books. Roger McCrow is our economics man, and apart from being an accountant, comes from Dawsons, whose Pall Mall business and address Pickering & Chatto acquired in 1982. This book contains the distillation of the knowledge of a team of colleagues, and I have them to thank for it. Opinions in the trade vary a great deal, and while *How to Buy Rare Books* may reflect the views of Pickering & Chatto it does not necessarily claim to represent the views of Christie's, the co-publishers.

The book market has its own contours. There are the broad plàins of second-hand' books, often sold for a few pounds or dollars – not rare, or not thought to be rare, often collected but not sold to collectors so much as bought by ordinary readers, or casual passers-by. There are the antiquarian slopes, old books of real interest, some of them rare, collected rather than bought casually, an important part of every good collection or library. Then there are the great rarities, the most important and valuable books, ranging up to the highest peaks, of which the First Folio of Shakespeare of 1623 is the most famous, but the Gutenberg Bible of about 1450–5, the first printed book, is the greatest of all. The highest price ever paid for any work of art at auction was in fact for a medieval manuscript, the Gospels of Henry the Lion, which sold for 8·14 million pounds in 1983. But we will not be discussing the collecting of manuscripts except where it is most closely allied to collecting printed books.

All the better bookdealers include a stock of interesting antiquarian books and also some of the landmarks of literary history. But even the greatest dealers and auction houses will sell some inexpensive second-hand books, because we all try to meet the interests of our customers, and value books by their contents not solely by their prestige or their prices.

Some of the books that we will be discussing are very rare and expensive. Obviously the ordinary collector will not be buying valuable works such as these, but it is natural to find them exciting, and they do make the best stories. The sale of a Shakespeare First Folio is a different matter from the sale of, say, a second edition of Evelyn Waugh's *Brideshead Revisited*, which might be had for a few pounds. Yet collecting even second editions of Evelyn Waugh might be an interesting and worthwhile thing to do. Certainly no collector should be put off by talk of the great books from buying good and interesting ones. The best should never be the enemy of the good.

It is possible to enjoy book collecting whatever the size of your budget, and to enjoy it both in the great bookshops and auction houses in the great cities of the world and at the bookstalls on the market corner. I hope this book will help people to develop that enjoyment.

William Rees-Mogg

1. *The Art and Practice of Book Collecting*

Duke Humfrey's Library at the Bodleian Library, Oxford.

Public libraries were rare in the fifteenth and sixteenth centuries. One such was Duke Humfrey's Library at Oxford, founded in the 1440s but later dispersed by theft and neglect. In 1602 the library was reopened in the name of a new benefactor, Sir Thomas Bodley, and the much-expanded collection is now the central library of the university.

WHY COLLECT BOOKS?

Book collecting is first and foremost an expression of love. Collectors are called *bibliophiles*, a word made up of two Greek words—*biblio*, which is the stem of the Greek word for book, and *phile*, which is the stem of the Greek word for love. Yet book collectors are not book lovers in any trifling or figurative sense. Their books are a focus of a deeply felt emotion, an expression of an important part of their personalities, an enlargement and an intensification of their lives.

Love for books is neither a mere fancy, nor, in its proper form, an attraction only to the physical object—to paper, black ink and brown leather, beautiful though books can be. It is a response to what John Milton wrote of in his tract *Areopagitica* (written in defence of a free press, and itself a most desirable book for collectors of English literature or of books concerned with the idea of liberty):

> Books are not absolutely dead things, but doe contain a potencie of life in them to be as active as that soule was whose progeny they are; nay they do preserve as in a violl the purest efficacie and extraction of that living intellect that bred them ... a good book is the pretious life-blood of a master spirit, imbalm'd and treasur'd upon purpose to a life beyond life.

Collecting books is not, therefore, a trivial pursuit. A collector should not think of himself as one who merely collects objects, things for their own sake, as one might collect stamps or cigarette cards. Almost all collectors begin like that—with the urge to complete a series, or to possess an author's works uniformly bound—but the true collector has a higher end in view: he is collecting both words and objects. In collecting the words he is taking the ideas and visions of other men or women into his own mind; and in collecting the objects he is collecting the history of the transmission of those words. To collect the works of a great writer is to absorb his whole: the framework of his ideas, his understanding of the world, his intellectual or imaginative power.

All book collectors run the risk of succumbing to that unhappy disease,
bibliomania—a dangerous addiction to books. Many are the collectors in
history who have indulged their passion beyond their means, sometimes
bringing ruin and unhappiness on their families. A few, like Richard
Heber (1773–1833) or Sir Thomas Phillipps (1792–1872), have filled their
houses so completely with books as to leave no room for human
habitation. Such are the dangers of uncontrolled collecting; but if you are
a new collector you should not be put off by the thought that you too
might be caught in this net, for the pursuit of fine and rare books can be
one of the joys of life. And for those able to restrain themselves it need not
be disastrously expensive.

Yet why should a book collector pay a hundred pounds or dollars for an
early edition of a book whose text he might obtain for a fraction of that
sum? Beauty may be one reason; sentiment or sentimentality another. But
the possession of an early edition, especially the first, of any book brings
to the reader a particular feeling of closeness with the author. Open the
little anonymous pamphlet publication of Alexander Pope's poem *The
Dunciad* (1728) and Pope seems to speak to you. The two great folio
volumes of Johnson's *Dictionary* (1755) bring Samuel Johnson closer than
any nineteenth-century reprint. The earliest editions of Shakespeare's
plays, hot from the stage, often provide corrupt texts, but they put the
reader just outside the stage door of the Globe Theatre.

It is natural that this should be so. Textual scholars may argue the

Samuel Pepys (1633–1703, pictured right) is best known for his diary, but to bibliophiles he is important for his library, which he bequeathed on his death to his nephew and thence to Magdalene College, Cambridge. The fine building which was built to hold his choice collection is shown above. Pepys's library contains many ephemeral publications which would otherwise not have survived, as well as many presentation copies from his famous contemporaries. By the terms of Pepys's will, no book may be sold from and none added to the library, and the collection is therefore unique as a private library which has not changed since the early eighteenth century.

merits or faults of a particular first edition, but the fact that it *is* the first, the earliest appearance before the world of that very text, the one the author would have seen and perhaps approved, exercises a special pull on the imagination of the collector. The original edition assists the process by which deeper layers of the mind take part in our reading of a significant book. We make a deeper response because the book in front of us helps us to make a closer association.

This is true in subjects other than literature. A few years ago a doctor from Galveston, Texas, paid a visit to a London antiquarian bookshop. 'I'm interested in Burns' he said, and the shop bustled with staff looking out editions of Robert Burns's poems. A row of Burns's books was placed on the table in front of him. 'No,' said the doctor, 'I said I was interested in *burns*', and so the medical books had to be sorted through. But for different collectors, Burns or burns, one for those fond of Scottish poetry, the other for surgeons who have treated victims of fire (and who are interested in the history of such treatment), are equally appropriate. What the collector must know is where his real interests lie, and that is as much a matter of emotion as of intellect. What really excites you? What makes your heart beat faster?

The second section of this book attempts to explain the attractions of some major collecting areas, and to suggest why the first edition of Copernicus's *De Revolutionibus* (1543) might be considered as exciting a book as the first edition of Wordsworth's and Coleridge's *Lyrical Ballads* (1798), or why the *Hypnerotomachia Poliphili* of Francesco Colonna (1499) might appeal to an art historian as much as Graunt's *Natural and Political Observations* (1662) to the historian of statistics. And what American remains unmoved at the sight of the Bay Psalm Book (1640), the first surviving book printed in the New World?

These books are not icons, however, to be considered alone in a barren landscape. No collection of the early editions of Shakespeare, for instance, would be complete without a copy of Sir Thomas North's translation of Plutarch's *Lives of the Noble Grecians and Romans* (1579), from which Shakespeare took the themes for his Roman plays; or the *Chronicles* of Raphael Holinshed (1587), from which he took many of the details for his plays on British history. Whether the collector interests himself in mathematics or fine bindings, in metallurgy or modern French literature, the broad base of his subject should not escape him. This is because all book collectors are, in a minor way, active historians of their subject, constantly on the lookout for additions to their sum of knowledge, conscious of their ability to illustrate through their library the progress and change of the subject they have chosen.

Let us suppose, for example, that you, the collector, had an interest in the plays of Shakespeare and a desire to make a collection based on them. Where do you begin your collection? About half of Shakespeare's plays and poems were first published in small quarto volumes between the years 1593 and 1622. They survive in very few copies; most of those copies are in public libraries; they are, when they appear on the market, keenly contested. So unless you are very young and very rich you will not have the time and means to acquire these quarto editions. The same is true of the first collected edition, the 'First Folio', published in 1623: although it is a relatively common book, judged by the number of copies which survive (something approaching 200), it is so sought-after by collectors and librarians that it has become the second most expensive printed book ever sold (if one excepts a collection of prints such as Audubon's *Birds of America*)—the highest prices having been attained by the first printed book, the 'Gutenberg Bible'.

So where does the collector of Shakespeare go for books obtainable at moderate prices? It is an axiom of book collecting that the more recent the book, the commoner it will be. Adapting to circumstances, as all collectors must learn to do, the searcher after Shakespearean texts could decide to investigate the subsequent history of Shakespearean drama—in the later seventeenth century, in the eighteenth or even in the nineteenth century. Needless to say, you will not be the first in the field but this is not without its advantages, since some bibliographies and catalogues of collections will be already available to you, and these will stake out the ground and could save many preliminary mistakes. H. L. Ford's bibliography of the

Michael Wodhull (1740–1816), the English collector, and his armorial on a book from his library.

Wodhull's books will become familiar to collectors of early books, for he had a large library and sold (in 1801 and 1803) many of his duplicates. The main library was sold by his descendants in 1886. His habit of picking the best leaves from two copies of the same book to make one better copy and one worse is frowned upon by today's collectors.

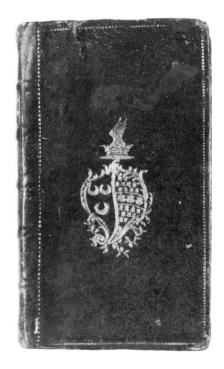

J. Pierpont Morgan (1837–1913) the multi-millionaire banker, who formed in the early years of this century a magnificent collection of exquisite books and manuscripts housed in his home in New York. The house is now a museum of the book, open to the public. Other great collections were being formed at the same time by Henry E. Huntington at San Marino, California, and by Henry Clay Folger at Washington, D.C. The Huntington and Folger Libraries are also now institutions open to scholars for research.

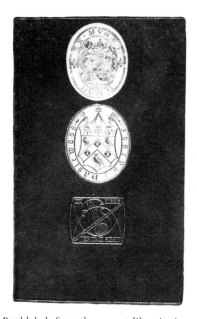

Booklabels from three great libraries in a copy of Richard Lovelace's *Lucasta*, London, 1649.

Joseph Haslewood (centre) was a founder-member of the Roxburghe Club: his library was sold on his death in 1833. The Huth library (top) was formed by Henry (1815–78) and Alfred Huth (1850–1910), and was one of the most comprehensive collections of early English literature formed in the nineteenth century. Jerome Kern (bottom), better known for his songs than for his book collection, formed a fine library of English books and manuscripts during the 1920s; it was sold at auction for spectacular prices just before the crash on Wall Street in 1929.

plays of Shakespeare, covering the years 1700–40 (published in 1935) shows how even a short period of publishing history can be full of interest. The nineteenth century, with all its vulgarization of Shakespearean ideals and proliferation of editions, is cheap to collect and largely unexplored. Granted, not even the possession of Samuel Johnson's edition (1765) could really impart a thrill comparable with owning a First Folio or an early quarto, but the collector must learn to make the best of the game as he finds it.

How to Begin

Beginning collecting is almost as mysterious as beginning breathing: where does the impulse come from? When does a random purchase of books turn into a collection? Many collectors have never thought of themselves as collectors at all, simply book buyers, and many great collections have begun life as nothing other than personal research libraries—necessary for the educated reader in the days when the great public libraries were in their infancy. Paintings, the book buyer might have said to himself, are for collectors; but books are for readers. On the other hand even if a conscious decision is made to keep to one subject, it is unlikely that the collection will have any coherence if the collector is not moved by a deeper impulse than the urge merely to collect. And every literate collector will also be impelled to stray from the path sometimes—as well may a cinema-goer proclaim that he only watches French films of the 1930s, or the musician only listen to Viennese waltzes, as the book collector try to exclude other subjects from his library. Collecting can be an infinite extension of the collector's personal interests, and the 'beginning' and 'end' can only be artificial boundaries.

Let us assume, however, that you have decided to crystallize your interests in a collection of books. Some basic questions about the world of book buying and collecting may need first to be answered, dissolving perhaps a few illusions and suggesting a few useful precepts.

The first lesson to be learnt is that there is no such thing as a fixed price for a book: not only are all booksellers likely to have different views on the value of a book, but every copy of a given book will differ slightly in condition—this one may have an inappropriate binding, that one may have an inscription in it from the author to a friend, the next may have some leaves torn or missing. Some booksellers may be more reliable or realistic in the valuations they put on their books, but fashion and scarcity play their part also in these value-judgements: to say that any one price is 'right' is to venture an opinion as personal as to say that one painting is 'worth' more than another.

The second point, in some ways similar to the first, is that there are no absolute standards of taste and design. The opinions of a collector or bookseller who has been long in the field will deserve better attention than those of someone who is just beginning. But collecting is not a science, it is an art: experience and technique can count only for so much, and the rest is instinct, taste and luck.

The third point is that book collecting is a social business, in which good manners and courtesy are valued by the participants. It is not, however, an especially gregarious pursuit, for one of the essential qualities of a book is that it cannot speak to more than one reader at a time. The golfer joins a golf club, the politician may join a debating society; but the book collector has no such need for social gatherings and may (if he wishes) indulge his delight in splendid isolation. So the number of societies for book collectors is small, and they are generally exclusive or formed around groups of friends. But it does not pay to be misanthropic or mean-spirited as a collector, especially in your dealings with booksellers: they will appreciate your courtesy and good custom, and will reward you with friendly advice and help. Making problems for those you deal with will only rebound on you. Remember that no one is compelling you to buy from any particular dealer, and that what seems expensive to you may be cheap by another customer's standards. Bookshops are not charitable organizations; they are in business to do business, and even a small purchase will be welcomed as an expression of interest and as an earnest of good intentions.

Many collectors learn these lessons by chance or by trial and error, and some never learn them at all; but since the formation of a collection should be a pleasurable experience, as well as an illuminating one, the collector should begin with an understanding of how to get the most from the book trade in the friendliest way.

You have decided, then, that you want to collect; you perhaps have an idea of the subject you would like to investigate. What is the next step? Almost all antiquarian booksellers issue catalogues from time to time, some depending on their catalogues more than others for their living. Write to a few of them, having first made sure that they sell the sort of book you want to find, and ask them to send you catalogues on the subjects you propose to collect. Most booksellers send their catalogues free; but they will drop you from their mailing-list after a while if you do not buy. Specify your interests as much as you can, whilst avoiding at first taking too narrow a line. If you say that you are interested only in the novels of Ernest Hemingway, the bookseller may offer you those only, although you may find with experience that other American authors of the same period tempt you, or that you want to extend your collection from there to English fiction, or earlier American novels—or bullfighting, or modern Spain, or any one of a hundred areas. Too restricted a definition will narrow the mind, defeating the first object of collecting.

Always remember that the wisest collectors make mistakes and you will make some too. You may change your mind about the scope or style of your collection, or the ambitions you have for it. Begin slowly, laying the foundations by finding out about the antiquarian book trade—a brief survey of its operations is given on pages 16–25—and learning about the way books have been constructed through the ages. The final section of this book will help with the rudiments, although whole libraries have been written on the history of the printed book. Until your collection has settled into its theme, and maybe even afterwards, you will find it useful to supplement your reference works by using the bibliography section of a large public or university library, for some works of reference are more expensive than the books they themselves describe, and building a collection of reference books can be a major drain on resources which could often be better put into the books themselves. Bibliographies and reference books take many forms, but the most useful books for collectors are those dealing with a particular author, genre or subject. A bibliography of the novelist Joseph Conrad, for example, will list and describe all the original and some later editions of his individual works, as well as his contributions to periodicals, with perhaps a section on the surviving manuscripts. Bibliographies of a particular subject—say navigation, or ornithology—will not usually be comprehensive but should always detail the earliest and most important books. When you have determined your pattern of collecting you will learn of the most useful bibliographies in your subject through notes in booksellers' catalogues: we have tried to indicate the best and most widely used in the note on further reading on pages 152–5.

In the end, a collection is determined by the character and developing interests of its owner. No two collectors are alike, though each will reflect the age and body of the time. And though we may cast envious eyes on the great collections of the past, which often now adorn national or university libraries, and lament the passing of an age when bargains seemed to leap out at even the most casual buyer, we should reflect that those collectors were often remarkable for rejecting many 'obvious' purchases and buying

'The Bibliophilist's Haunt' by Sir William Douglas. This is an imaginative reconstruction of Creech's in Edinburgh, the famous eighteenth-century bookshop at the top of the High Street where for over a century literary men as well as bibliophiles gathered. William Creech (1745–1815) was, like so many other booksellers of his time, a publisher as well as a dealer.

what their contemporaries thought dull or worthless. A good collection contains not merely books which one's contemporaries will covet, but those which perhaps only future generations will value as much as you yourself do. The bargains are still there. As the late John Carter used to say, 'In book collecting, it's not the early bird who catches the worm, but the bird who knows a worm when he sees one.' And what higher ambition can the collector have than to store up riches for future generations to appreciate?

THE ANTIQUARIAN BOOK TRADE

All of us have an idea of the perfect antiquarian bookshop—something out of Dickens, perhaps, with an owner as venerable and dusty as the books he sells, with a cat forever sleeping on the window-sill (in winter, by a blazing fire in the back room), and priceless treasures locked carefully away in the basement. Occasionally these time-hallowed portals will see money change hands and a satisfied customer leave with the very book he was looking for—but mostly the actual *selling* of books seems an irrelevance, and the proprietor, in his Dickensian way, never grows older or ill-tempered but remains year after year his cherubic self, presiding over a never-changing establishment.

Such a shop may have existed once, somewhere. It is the bookshop we are all looking for, and indeed many booksellers do all they can to cultivate such an atmosphere in their shops, for if a bookshop is not pleasant to browse in, who will visit it? It would be unthinkable for

The premises of Messrs. William H. Robinson in London, just before the Second World War. Calculated to appeal only to the most distinguished customers, the Robinson shop's ambience is both businesslike and relaxed. Books in glass cases on the left are displayed for the casual customer to look at without touching, whilst more important clients would be taken into the back quarters or into the vault to be shown the treasures of the establishment.

antiquarian bookshops to become like supermarkets or fast-food restaurants, where it would no longer be necessary or desirable for the shopkeeper to maintain good relations with his customers. The experience of buying books has always been an enjoyable one and visiting bookshops should be, for the book collector, one of life's great pleasures.

Throughout the English-speaking world there are antiquarian bookshops of all kinds—the large and grandiose, the select and unwelcoming, the friendly and unpretentious. And there are innumerable types of book auction, ranging from the small section of books in a general sale in a provincial town to the grandest and most expensive specialist sale at one of the great houses in London or New York. Anyone who spends time travelling and visits bookshops *en route* will be aware that the diversity of booksellers and their ways of doing business are as broad and as long as humanity itself. No generalization could encompass the trade of bookselling—it is not even safe to assume that all booksellers like reading—so even the broadest of outlines will not prepare the collector for the surprises which contact with the trade will bring. (Is this unlikely little shop really the best place to buy fine bindings? Does that scruffy man really know the points of a Thackeray first edition by heart?) The most important rules, however, are those which the collector learns over many years, sometimes to his or her own cost but always with some benefit to the collection itself—and that, after all, is the most important thing.

The following description, then, is intended to give the collector a rough idea of how the book trade works, and to indicate the part the dealers and auctioneers play in it. Whilst there are many differences between Great Britain and North America, there is much more that unites the two communities of book collectors than divides them. The recent establishment and growth of the two old London auction houses in New York has only emphasized what has always been an established fact for bibliophiles of both nations: that, as far as book collecting is concerned, *Amor librorum nos unit* ('Love of books unites us', the motto of the International League of Antiquarian Booksellers).

Booksellers and Bookshops

For as long as there have been books, there have been book collectors, and where there are collectors, there will always be a trade to cater for them. The distinction between booksellers who deal in old and second-hand books and those who sell only new publications is, however, relatively recent. Until the beginning of this century, indeed, almost every bookseller handled both new and old books. Many were also publishers— and binders, stationers, and general suppliers of all sorts of equipment associated with books. To understand the book trade of four, two, or even one hundred years ago, we have to forget the modern classifications and imagine a world in which booksellers were catering on a wider scale to a much smaller range of customers. The bookseller in sixteenth-century London, Paris, or Amsterdam was primarily a printer and publisher, with his press and his stock all on the premises, but his customers would probably expect him to know about books in general—what were the best editions of certain authors, and where they could be obtained. Some traders also imported books from the great printing centres such as Venice or Basle, and became known for their expertise in certain types of book. But they all, especially the larger shops, dealt in books of many kinds.

Today, with the great explosion of printing and publishing, it is scarcely possible for the large bookshops to cover the whole range of new publications, let alone all the types of book ever published. Many

The trade ticket of Robert Paske, pasted into a copy of Ogilvy's *Africa* (1670). Paske was a publisher and bookseller, a binder and perhaps a printer as well. This engraved ticket, an early form of advertising, was among the surprises uncovered by the sale of the library of John Evelyn, the friend and contemporary of Samuel Pepys, at Christie's, London, in 1977–8.

Thomas Rowlandson, *Bookseller and Author*, c.1780–4. Pen and watercolour.

Up until the nineteenth and even into the twentieth century the bookseller was commonly a publisher as well as a shopkeeper. He would also be expected to keep old as well as new books in stock, and his shop would be a meeting-place for literary men. For the author, the bookseller was a terrible figure, to be revered in the same way that editors are feared by their authors today.

Ticknor's bookshop in Boston, Massachusetts, from a drawing of about 1835. William Davis Ticknor (1810–64) was a friend of Nathaniel Hawthorne and the leading publisher of his time in New England. He was also a bookseller, and (as the picture shows) his shop had a bindery on the upper floors.

The Green Knight Bookshop in St. Martin's Court, London.

Smaller bookshops such as this depend greatly on passing trade, but they will also have a number of regular customers who know the books they specialize in. Almost all booksellers refine their stock nowadays, because a broad and general stock in a city location is difficult to justify economically, but in bookshops such as this you may find any sort of book if you look hard enough.

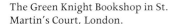

antiquarian bookshops keep a general stock of a varied type, but the traditional second-hand bookseller is an endangered species. This is partly caused by the enormous rise in the cost of keeping a large stock, but also perhaps by the increasing demands of his customers for particular expert knowledge, which means that the bookseller has to concentrate his business on the subjects and the periods he knows best. Many booksellers today are, or could be, academics in their own right. As in many another discipline or trade, they have had to specialize and streamline—or go under.

How does a book dealer run his business? The shop, where the casual customer can drop in and have a browse, is still the basis of the trade, but many booksellers, usually the highly specialized ones, operate only from their homes, sending out catalogues and dealing almost exclusively by post. This is possible because of the nature of their wares rather than misanthropy (though it may be a bit of both): books, unlike pictures, can be safely bought without being seen. If you are a collector of, say, books printed by the great Birmingham printer John Baskerville (1706–75), you can order a book printed by him from a bookseller's catalogue and have a pretty good idea of what it will look like. And if it turns out to be not what you expected, or if it has been wrongly described, then you can send it back to the bookseller. Nothing can replace the experience of having seen it, but the fact that every book, by the nature of the printing process, exists in more than one copy means that it is often possible for the bookseller to describe his ware by referring to a published description of another copy or, if his is peculiar or unique, by saying how his copy differs from others.

Do booksellers make profits? To hear some of them talk, you might think they never did. But it is in fact true that none of the wealthiest booksellers became rich through bookselling, for in their trade every deal is negotiated separately and cannot be repeated. An oil tycoon may discover a new well which will produce money for him over many years; an author may write a book which sells edition after edition; an inventor or industrialist may find a new product line which retains its popularity down the years. The bookseller may, it is true, make some deals which are

ABOVE
Beach's bookshop, Salisbury, Wiltshire, is housed in a fine half-timbered building. Many bookshops, especially in English provincial towns, sell topographical prints, which are a great favourite with tourists and residents alike and may come from broken books in stock. English towns are full of interesting bookshops with surprisingly large stocks—the sort of shop which used to exist in London until property prices made the cost of keeping a larger shop prohibitive.

Jacob Zeitlin, doyen of the Californian book trade, outside his shop in Los Angeles. Jake made his way from Fort Worth to Los Angeles in 1927 to set up business as a bookseller. His appreciation of good printing and contemporary verse has done much to encourage the modern Californian supremacy in fine book production, but he is equally at home with great scientific books or incunabula.

Bernard Quaritch (1819–99) came from his native Saxony to London in 1842, and found employment in the bookshop of H. G. Bohn. In 1847 he set up on his own and for the rest of the century his reputation steadily increased so that by his death he was the most famous, as well as the most powerful and discriminating, antiquarian dealer in the world. He bought and sold no less than six copies of the Gutenberg Bible during his forty years of bookselling, and his firm continues today as a major presence in the international market.

of immense value to him, but these are not recurring profit makers and they are often a matter of chance; they also have to be used to tide him over the lean times when nothing seems to go right. Every sale that he makes is unique, and in the small world which dealers inhabit, no sale can be taken for granted.

The survival and success of any book-dealing business, then, is a matter of hard work in which attention to the quality of the stock and to the requirements of the customers are the bookseller's paramount considerations. To begin trading the dealer must not only know his subject matter but he must also have a good stock of books to trade with: if he has no stock but only the knowledge he will become a 'runner' (a bookseller who buys only for a quick resale, generally to another dealer); if he has the stock but no knowledge he will soon become a bankrupt.

The amount of 'mark up' which a bookseller puts on a purchase varies widely, and legend often places it at exorbitant rates. In fact, booksellers' mark up is related to speed of turnover: a book bought on commission will have a 10 per cent commission charge because it is sold as soon as bought;

CATALOGUS
Variorum & Infignium
LIBRORUM
Inftructiffimæ Bibliothecæ

Clariffimi Doctiffimiq; Viri

LAZARI SEAMAN, S.T.D.

Quorum Auctio habebitur *L O N D I N I*
in ædibus Defuncti in Area & Viculo
Warwicenfi, Octobris ultimo.

Cura *GULIELMI COOPER* Bibliopolæ.

L O N D I N I,
Apud { Ed. Brewfter & Guil. Cooper } ad Infigne { Gruis in Cæmiterio *Paulino,* Pelicani in Vico vulgariter dicto *Little-Britain.* } 1676.

The sale of Lazarus Seaman's library in 1676 was the first auction to be held in England. The conditions of sale were strikingly similar to those employed in all major auction rooms today.

a book bought in expectation of a quick sale might have a 30 per cent margin (like that of a seller of new books); a book held in stock for several years may eventually be sold for a multiple of its original price. Since most bookdealers have a very slow turnover, this is not such a dramatic price-increase as it seems: a book may sit on the shelves for several years, waiting for the right customer to find it, and by this time the money invested in the book will have been eaten up by inflation or interest charges, and by the basic cost of keeping the shop open. It should be stressed, however, that few booksellers will sell something to a customer cheaply just because they have managed to buy it for almost nothing. Finding such bargains is, after all, their profession; and, as one famous contemporary American dealer has a habit of saying: 'If I find a five dollar bill on the street, does that mean I should sell it to you for two dollars?'

The Auction Houses

The sale of books at auction is always an occasion: as with the sale of pictures and furniture, it is only at auction that the passions that fine books can arouse are seen in public. Even at the smallest provincial sale a battle royal may develop between two bidders—or a valuable article pass unnoticed. Every regular auction-goer has a tale to tell, and three hundred years of book auctions have left their mark on collecting history: indeed, famous sales have changed attitudes and marked ends of eras in collecting.

The first sale of a library at auction in England was held in 1676; it dispersed the collection of Dr Lazarus Seaman. But the great age of the

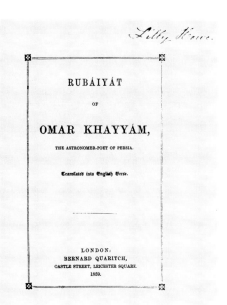

Rubaiyat of Omar Khayyam, translated by Edward Fitzgerald, London, Bernard Quaritch, 1859.

First published in an edition of 250 copies by Bernard Quaritch, the antiquarian bookseller, copies of Fitzgerald's translation of the *Rubaiyat* were remaindered at one penny each when they sold slowly. Quaritch's firm made amends in 1979, however, when they bought this copy for £4,620 ($8,775) at the Houghton sale at Christie's, London.

auctioneer was the eighteenth century, when most of the leading London houses of today were founded. Samuel Baker, a bookseller who turned his hand to the book auction business, is traditionally said to have founded his business in 1744. Through various changes of ownership Baker's firm evolved into the present-day Sotheby's, whose business until almost the middle of this century still centred on the sale of books at auction. James Christie founded his business in 1766, and with his silver-tongued oratory (a very important talent for an auctioneer at that time) became the best-known auctioneer in London. Among the famous libraries sold by him and by his son, also James, were those of Dr Johnson (in 1785) and Queen Charlotte (in 1818). But it was as an auctioneer of paintings and jewellery that Christie's became famous, and it is only since the Second World War

Robert Dighton's caricature of the first James Christie (1730–1803), eloquent auctioneer and founder of the present-day firm. When he began his business, Christie sold almost anything (even loads of hay) but he soon concentrated on fine art, including books and prints.

THE SPECIOUS ORATOR.
WILL YOUR LADYSHIP DO ME THE HONOR TO SAY /30.000
— A MERE TRIFLE — A BRILLIANT of the FIRST WATER,
an unheard of price for such a lot, surely.

A book auction in 1888, at Sotheby's. Bernard Quaritch sits below the auctioneer; other dealers and *habitués* of the rooms sit round the table. To the auctioneer's right sits the clerk, taking the names and noting the price of each lot. On the far right, seated, is Frederick Locker-Lampson, poet and book collector.

that Christie's has established regular book sales and has become a major presence in the book market.

For the collector, what purpose does the present-day auction house serve? Perhaps its most obvious function is to disperse the large private collections which dealers generally cannot handle. Until recent times almost every literate individual of means would gather a private library of significant value; as often as not, this would be sold at auction after his or her death in a special sale devoted to that collection. Today, the flow of books is quite as large, but for a variety of reasons—not the least being the steep rise in overheads for auctioneers—sales confined to one collection are usually accorded only to the most important and valuable libraries, and most auction sales are now a mixture of properties. Within the trade, book sales are regarded as a vital source of 'new' books—that is, books which have not been seen on the open market for many years. Of course, since the bookdealer and the auctioneer are frequently competing against each other for the same books it would be astonishing if there were not occasionally some ill feeling between them. But generally speaking, the two forces co-exist in friendly competition for the custom of vendors: the auction houses maintaining a lead in the handling of large collections and the dealers in the application of special expertise.

For the vendor, however, the essential point about an auction house is that it is an invaluable market-place for realizing the best, or at least a fair, price for a book—or for any collectable object. It is partly because of the auction houses' success in the last fifty years that dealers have grown to be more specialized: the result is that most of the very valuable books which come on the market are handled by auction houses, and are bought at auction by specialized dealers acting on behalf of collectors.

Auctions are also important for the publicity they bring to the sale of books. This is not just a matter of advertising: it is useful to every collector to know that certain types of book are increasing in value, or that they are becoming harder to sell. The wise collector, like the good dealer, will study the auctions, and watch out not merely for the books which interest him but also for the general trend in prices. A subscription to the catalogues of the principal auctions in London and New York—with perhaps an eye kept on the catalogues of country sales near your home—is a useful investment for the beginner as much as for the experienced collector.

HOW TO READ A CATALOGUE

'Not in Greg'; 'pagination and running-title shaved'; 'final gathering sprung'; 'collation differing from GKW 2314'—such notes lie scattered throughout catalogues of books offered for sale by both dealers and auctioneers. Like any specialization—it would hardly be wrong to call it a science—the description of books for sale is well supplied with terms which mean very little to the layman, but whose use is fraught with significance for the initiated. It would be impossible to unlock the mystery of all these terms in one brief chapter, and in any event the best teacher is experience since there are many terms which are either obsolete or used so rarely (or used in the description of books so unusual as to be hardly ever encountered) that learning them by rote would simply be a waste of time. Special terms are merely tools for the understanding of the physical object; they should not be thought of as incantatory symbols with a significance divorced from the books themselves.

The catalogue is of particular importance to the antiquarian bookseller, since it is both his advertisement and his means of trading. A number of dealers—often the best and most sophisticated—never bother to issue catalogues; but the majority will publish one or two a year at least, if only as a self-discipline. The special appropriateness of selling books through the medium of books (akin to selling televisions by television) is not lost on the trade, and many dealers and historians of the book trade form collections of catalogues. The most notable was perhaps Seymour de Ricci (1881–1942), a prodigiously energetic and knowledgeable bibliographer and collector, whose library of book catalogues was said to be rivalled only by that in the Bibliothèque Nationale in Paris—and, very appropriately, de Ricci bequeathed it on his death to that very library.

Early auction catalogues are also avidly sought after by both booksellers and collectors, partly because they are more informative than catalogues of, for instance, jewellery, but partly also because the sale catalogue of the library of a famous man tells us things about him which we would otherwise never have known. Sometimes the fortunate collector can trace a particular copy of a particular book through famous sales for two centuries or more. Booksellers also take a special pride in the antiquity of book auctions, which are certainly better recorded by historians, and are probably older, in any regular form, than auctions of any other kind of collectable object.

What, then, are the basic rules for reading a book catalogue? First of all it is necessary to be aware of some of the traditions which govern the book trade and which are revealed in the cataloguing styles of different institutions. Why should it be true, for instance, that auction catalogues, which have a wide circulation, will often deal so briefly with books worth thousands of pounds? Like so many matters concerning the book trade, this is a matter of custom and convenience, and it rapidly becomes a commonplace for the book buyer.

Reading an Auction Catalogue

Bearing in mind what has already been said about sales at auction, a most important fact to remember about the catalogues is that the auctioneer can only sell what he has been requested to sell: whilst he may wish to offer the bidders a selection of, say, nineteenth-century novels, he can only do so if a client asks him to sell some. The bookseller who wishes to sell a particular type of book can go out and buy some, and then write a catalogue of them; but unless the auctioneer is asked to sell a large and coherent collection, the catalogue he compiles is always likely to be somewhat random in its composition. The best auctioneers will always try to combine in the same sale the same sorts of book—just as they will avoid selling Old Masters in the same sale as English watercolours—for they know by experience that a sale full of, for example, medical books will attract the main collectors and dealers in that subject, and that a very mixed sale will only confuse the customers. It is the very unpredictability of the goods brought for auction that is often the charm of the catalogues. You can never tell what you might come across—it may be a wonderful association copy of an important book, or it may be a tired example of a standard book seen a hundred times before.

Because the auctioneer is acting as a broker between the vendor and the purchaser his most important duty is to make sure that there are no essential mistakes in the description of the book he is offering. All good auctioneers guarantee that their descriptions are correct, and they will accept the book as returned goods, within a specified period, if the buyer can prove the description to have been inaccurate in some important detail. This has been true from the very first book auctions and remains a condition fundamental to book sales today. Whilst the same is true of booksellers, who will also accept the return of a book— and often for less reason—the auctioneer is in a special position of responsibility, for no owner likes to be told that the book which he thought had been sold yesterday is today no longer sold. Consequently the auctioneer will take extra care to ensure that none of the book's faults is omitted from the catalogue description.

Furthermore, the special tradition of auction houses dictates that the auctioneer does not 'cry up' his wares, but leaves it to the enthusiasm of those present to create the price. This is a relatively recent tradition: auction catalogues of the eighteenth century tended to lavish superlatives on the best books and manuscripts, and witnesses tell us that the auctioneer on his rostrum was even more grandiloquent. But the habit

A

CATALOGUE

OF THE VALUABLE

Library of Books,

Of the late learned

SAMUEL JOHNSON,

Efq; LL. D.

DECEASED;

Which will be Sold by Auction,

(By ORDER of the EXECUTORS)

By Mr. CHRISTIE,

At his Great Room in Pall Mall,

On WEDNESDAY, FEBRUARY 16, 1785,

AND THREE FOLLOWING DAYS.

To be Viewed on Monday and Tuefday preceding the Sale, which will begin each Day at 12 o'Clock.

Catalogues may be had as above.

Samuel Johnson's library was sold by Christie's two months after his death. In the eighteenth century fewer lots were offered in each session, and the 662 lots in this sale took four days to sell. Only fourteen copies of the catalogue are known: the last copy to sell at auction fetched $8,800 (£4,170) at Christie's, New York, in 1981.

Phillipps's sales were a regular feature of the London salerooms in the 1960s and early 1970s. Sotheby's series of auctions uncovered some astonishing finds: in this sale the missing half of the only known manuscript of Caxton's translation of Ovid sold for £90,000 to a New York dealer.

The sale of some choice items from the library of Arthur A. Houghton, jun., at Christie's in 1979–80 was the grandest sale of English literature in recent years. The books on offer included all four folios of Shakespeare and the original manuscript of Gilbert White's *Natural History of Selborne*.

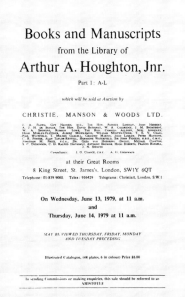

faded with the rise in the nineteenth century of a professional body of antiquarian booksellers: men whose business it was to attend auctions, and who preferred to make up their own mind about the quality and importance of what was on offer. It remains true today that most bidding at auction is done by dealers, although they may frequently be acting on behalf of customers. So, whilst a private collector may appreciate a note of personal enthusiasm in a catalogue entry, a bidder who has seen a hundred copies of, say, Ackermann's *Microcosm of London* (1808–10) does not want or need to be told that it is one of the most attractive collections of coloured aquatint illustrations of London scenes published in the nineteenth century: such an opinion would be superfluous and perhaps controversial. This does not mean that it is impossible for a private collector to buy at auction (although many dealers prefer to have the field to themselves), but a situation which is already full of traps for the unwary can be made more difficult by the brevity of the descriptions and the frequent use of jargon and abbreviations.

The private buyer also has to remember that once the hammer comes down the book is sold irrevocably: you cannot return it if you change your mind or decide that the price was too high. Only a serious error in description will allow you to send it back, so strong nerves and sharp wits are needed to bid at auction (see pp. 32–6).

To show the standard style of cataloguing one might expect in an auction catalogue, here is a typical lot in a recent London sale of illustrated books.

46 EGAN (PIERCE): LIFE IN LONDON, or the day and night scenes of Jerry Hawthorn, Esq., FIRST ISSUE OF THE FIRST EDITION, *without footnote on p. 9, 3 engraved folding sheets of music, the first unnumbered, half-title (but no advert leaves at end), 36 handcoloured engraved plates by I. R. and G. Cruikshank, red morocco gilt, pugilistic motif within compartments gilt on spine, inner dentelles, g.e., [Abbey: Life 281; Cohn 262; Tooley 196], 8vo, 1821*

£150–200

When *Life in London* was published in 1821 its success was immediate, for both text and illustrations are amusing and inventive; but it is as an example of the art of George Cruikshank, one of the most talented English humorous artists of the nineteenth century, that it is collected today. The cataloguer has, however, used the standard auction-house style in listing the book—lot 46—under its author, and has then transcribed the most important part of the title page. Immediately after the title comes the edition, a crucial piece of information: is this the first edition or a subsequent one? And if it is the first edition, are there any special points about it? In this instance, the answer to both questions is yes: this is an early issue of the first edition, printed and published before an extra footnote was added at the bottom of page 9. So this copy is somewhat more collectable than a copy of the later issue, and the relevant details are put in small capitals for emphasis.

The rest of the description, set in italics, contains information about the physical state of the book. The illustrations are usually the only part of the inside of the book to receive special mention, although as the half-title and the concluding advertisements are frequently missing in books that have been re-bound the catalogue specifies which are present in this copy. If any text or essential part of the book is missing, the catalogue must say so, or the purchaser is entitled to return it as wrongly described. After the listing of the number of plates, the catalogue describes the binding. In this case the alert reader will notice that the description of the binding does not specify its age—almost always a bad sign, since contemporary binding would be worth mentioning, and one would look for a book in its original condition if possible. Usually a cataloguer will avoid dating a binding when he thinks it would detract from the book or when its age is a matter for debate—or when the binding is of such decrepitude or plainness as to be irrelevant. Here the binding sounds as though it is of the early twentieth century, and it has a decoration on its spine to show the theme of the book (although boxing is not the only subject of *Life in London*). The dentelles and the gilt edges ('g. e.') to the leaves further suggest to the experienced reader how the book will look. But the experienced collector as well as the beginner will need to see the book before the sale, and should always attend the view; never bid on a book you have not seen.

After the description of the inside of the book and its binding, the catalogue gives a list of references to bibliographies. These references will mean nothing to the inexperienced reader but are of great use to the potential buyer, since the three bibliographies mentioned provide reliable descriptions of what a copy of the first edition of *Life in London* ought to contain, and the reader can check this copy against the entry before the sale and, if he buys it, afterwards. For the collector of books illustrated by Cruikshank the most important of these three is Cohn: this means that the book is no. 262 in Albert M. Cohn's *George Cruikshank: A Catalogue Raisonné* (1924), the standard work on this artist's illustrative work. The other two references are to J. R. Abbey's *Life in England in Aquatint and Lithography 1770–1860* (London, 1953, reprint 1972), which catalogues a famous collection of illustrated books, and R. V. Tooley's *English Books with Coloured Plates 1790–1860* (London, 1954, reprinted 1973, revised

---

FIFTEENTH-CENTURY BOOKS
ILLUSTRATING THE SPREAD OF PRINTING

The Collection of
the late Eric Sexton, F.S.A.
and
Seventeen Duplicates from
The Pierpont Morgan Library

which will be sold on
WEDNESDAY, APRIL 8, 1981
at 10:00 a.m.

VIEWING

This sale may be viewed only by prior appointment with Christie's
Book Department at the following times

Wednesday, April 1 to Saturday, April 4, from 10:00 a.m. to 4:30 p.m. and on
Tuesday, April 7, from 10:00 a.m. to 2:00 p.m. (closed Sunday and Monday)

In sending bids or making enquiries, this sale should be referred to as
SEXTON—5046

CHRISTIE, MANSON & WOODS INTERNATIONAL INC.
502 Park Avenue • New York, N.Y. 10022
Telephone: (212) 546-1000 • Cables: Chriswoods, New York • International Telex: New York 620 721

Eric Sexton was an Englishman who emigrated to the United States: his library was sold in both London and New York in 1981, with the incunabula making New York's most important auction of early books for many years.

1979), a useful one-volume guide to the best English illustrated books of that period.

In a place of prominence at the end of the description are three essential pieces of information: the format of the book, its date and the estimate for the lot. The reader who is familiar with the book will of course be well aware of the size and date of the first edition, but it is important to have confirmation that this copy is the same. The estimate is also useful—though estimates often prove wrong in practice, and the buyer should always make up his own mind before the bidding rather than rely on the sometimes pessimistic auction house suggestion of what the lot might fetch. Estimates are sometimes printed separately from the lots, on an inserted sheet or at the end of the catalogue, and in provincial auction rooms it is common for no estimate to be provided at all.

Because auction catalogues often contain the property of many different sellers, the compilers will sometimes arrange the lots not simply by subject, but also by owner. This is not done unless the owner or the books are of unusual interest or distinction. If Mr Smith of Newtown sells a book of average value it will not be separated from the main alphabetical run of the catalogue. If, on the other hand, the Countess of Blank sells a few books from her country house it is possible that her books will be put in a special position of prominence, even if they are not of exceptional value: books from old or noble collections are always of greater interest to buyers—and this is not mere snobbery, for whilst the Countess's finances may be under strain, her ancestors' pockets are likely to have been deep, and the books in her library will have been bought as good copies, and often bound in finer bindings than usual. Thus the noble vendor's books are likely to be prefaced in the catalogue by some formula such as: 'The Property of the Countess of Blank, from the Library at Blank Hall, Blankshire.'

Some owners—especially when valuable property is being sold—prefer to remain anonymous, and on these occasions the phrases 'The property of a gentleman' and 'The property of a lady' will be used, with variations. These terms, while meaningless in themselves, are sometimes useful to buyers because they indicate that the book is from a genuine private library, and that it is not being sold for a dealer who could not find a buyer himself.

American auction houses tend to be less concerned about indicating the provenance in this way, and catalogues are commonly more rigorously alphabetical and divided by subject. This is not because American buyers do not care about the provenance of the books they buy—far from it—but because there is very little selling of books from dealers' stocks in American auction houses: the label 'Various Properties' therefore will mean private consignment for the most part. The American method is to identify the important consignors whenever possible. At Christie's in New York a recent sale of printed and manuscript documents from the papers of the Chew family, a colonial American family of distinction, whose collection included the original drawing for the Mason-Dixon line and a copy of the first printing of the Declaration of Independence (1776), received the accolade of a separate catalogue with the Chew arms embossed on the cover.

Dealers' catalogues come in all sizes, on all subjects, and from all the great bookselling centres of the world.

Reading a Bookseller's Catalogue

Auctioneers may vary in their style of compiling catalogues, but the basic method is generally very similar. Booksellers, however, have a hundred ways of describing a book, and as they are unconstrained by the need to act on anyone's behalf but their own they will emphasize different aspects according to their personal taste. In size, in lavishness or economy of printing, and most of all in approach, the bookseller's catalogue is often very different from that of the auctioneer. The bigger booksellers may produce from time to time, perhaps twice or three times a year, a large catalogue advertising their more expensive books on various subjects; lesser catalogues, more cheaply produced, may be interspersed as required. A thick catalogue from some of the major booksellers is an event: often some years of preparation will have gone into the buying and cataloguing, and the fact that the books are for sale seems almost less important than the catalogue's publicity value. The bookseller is not merely showing that he has these books for sale; he is making a point about the quality and distinction of his stock in general.

The immediate provenance of the books listed in a bookseller's catalogue is usually of little interest, since he is the owner of all the books described. His catalogues will therefore usually be strictly divided into subjects, since his aim is to help his customers find the books they want. A catalogue compiled at random, or full of misprints, or typed illegibly, will put his customers off.

Searching a catalogue for the sort of books you collect requires a technique similar to 'speed-reading': much of the catalogue may be of little interest, and maintaining one's concentration is difficult, so the collector must keep his wits about him and look out for key words or names. Yet the serendipitous browse in a catalogue can be as delightful as an afternoon in a bookshop; and you will doubtless learn about other books and prices as you go along, so do not let any catalogue go unread: the very book you have been searching for, at a price you think a bargain, may lie within.

Learning the bookseller's jargon is something which comes with time, and a reading of the glossary to this book (pp.144–8) will, we hope, provide some of the information the buyer needs, for nothing in the collecting of books is more useful—and, generally speaking, more undervalued—than a good understanding of how old books were constructed. Without at least a working knowledge of the history of printing, the book collector can only half understand the significance of his library, and the technical language with which book catalogues are filled will be a meaningless babble.

BUYING AND SELLING

Buying from a dealer

Once you start to receive catalogues from a few dealers and you have visited a few shops, you will begin to find books that interest you, perhaps books that you want to buy. How do you go about making a purchase? If you were buying a pint of milk or a loaf of bread, you would produce the money there and then; but with a valuable book it may not be so easy to find the money immediately. Most dealers allow at least a week or two's credit—but only to customers they already know. Unless they are satisfied that you are credit-worthy, they will not dispatch a book to you or let you take if from the shop without prepayment. But usually they will reserve it for you for a week or two, to allow time for payment (or for you to decide whether you can really afford it). Remember that it is not good manners to have the bookseller put aside books which you do not really want, or in which you have only a slight interest. This is especially true of books appearing in a new catalogue, for the bookseller may well have other orders for them, and he will not be best pleased if you pick and choose whilst five other potential buyers come and go. That said, booksellers always want to help their customers and you will usually find a sympathetic response if you cannot make up your mind.

A new catalogue will always bring a flood of orders to a bookshop, and if you delay in reading or deciding to order you may find that the book has gone. Whether buying at auction (see below) or from a dealer, it pays to make quick decisions. And do not harbour regrets afterwards: you may get a chance to buy another copy another day—perhaps more cheaply, or when your enthusiasm has cooled you may be relieved that you did not spend so lavishly. The lesson therefore must be to read all catalogues quickly, as soon as they come out, and place your order straightaway. In these days of instant communication it is best to telephone your order—even a transatlantic call is worth its cost if you make your point quickly and clearly. Almost all catalogues carry a number so that the bookseller knows which catalogue you are referring to (he may have issued several recently); and the books within will be numbered. Books in a catalogue are often referred to as 'items'—the term 'lot' is used only in an auction—for they may be autograph letters, literary manuscripts, long runs of periodicals, or something else not readily described as a book. Specify the catalogue you are referring to, and ask whether the items you want are still available. The bookseller will be keeping a master copy of the catalogue to hand, and the items already sold will have been crossed off. You will then know instantly what you may still buy, and the bookseller will note your order and (if you have already bought from him) dispatch the books to you with the invoice.

Check the books carefully when they arrive and, if you are happy with them, pay the invoice within a short time. Returning books to your dealer for petty reasons, or after a long period, is frowned upon, as is late payment: remember that you will get the best out of your dealer if you act in a responsible way. But if you discover that the book is incomplete, or has been misleadingly described, or is in some other way not what you expected, you are within your rights to return it and have your money refunded. In theory this right extends indefinitely, whether you have paid in cash or by cheque; but any bookseller will look unfavourably on you if you return a book more than a month or two after the sale.

From whom should you buy? As we have already indicated, there is no single standard by which booksellers may be judged. But in various countries the most reputable dealers have combined to form associations which maintain trading standards. Whilst this cannot insure you against your own folly, it can at least give you an assurance against malpractice on the part of the dealer. In Britain there is the Antiquarian Booksellers' Association; in the United States, the Antiquarian Booksellers' Association of America; and there are others in Canada and Australasia. Most other western countries have similar associations (a fuller list, with addresses, is given on pp.149–51), and they will be happy to send you a list of their members with their specialities. Almost all belong to the International League of Antiquarian Booksellers (I.L.A.B.). The national organizations have no legal powers, and they are often criticized as ineffective, but expulsion from his national association (the ultimate sanction) is a mark of disrepute which no antiquarian bookseller is likely to live down, and as it is a serious step it is rarely used.

Buying at Auction

Even the most casual reader of auction room notes in the newspapers will have seen mention of 'mystery' bidders and of dealers buying 'on behalf of' private collectors or public institutions. Why is this secrecy necessary or desirable? And why should buyers use dealers to carry out the simple act of bidding at auction? The first thing to be said is that the process of

The insignia or logos of the Antiquarian Booksellers' Association (the British national association), and Antiquarian Booksellers Association of America, and the International League of Antiquarian Booksellers.

ARTHUR HOE   DR.W.A.ROSENBACH   H. EISEMANN   MAJOR E.J.TURNER   ARTHUR SWAN   GEORGE D. SMITH   DR. GIUSEPPE MARTINI   ROBERT ROSE

Caricatures of dealers and collectors at the sale of the library of Robert Hoe in New York in 1912, from the *New York Herald Tribune*. George D. Smith, Huntington's representative, is third from the right; the great Dr Rosenbach, who was to succeed him, is second from the left.

Being an auctioneer was not always so glamorous: in the nineteenth century (as occasionally today) auctions might be held in the street by traders anxious for a quick sale. Here the book auctioneer is placed on a par with the Baked Potato Man (see p. 102) by Henry Mayhew in his *London Labour and the London Poor* (1851–2).

buying at auction is far from simple, easy though it may be to raise your hand to bid in a sale: whether you are buying in Glasgow or London, New York or Dallas, Munich or Montreal, an expert eye is always needed to pick out the gold from the dross. Remember that auctioneers have a dual role to play—to get the highest price for their vendor, and to see fair play in the competition for his property. And although they are concerned to provide a fair description for each lot, the old motto holds good: *caveat emptor* ('let the buyer beware'). Books should therefore be examined ('viewed') before the sale, and checked afterwards, for the speed at which the auctioneers have to produce catalogues means that their researches cannot be exhaustive.

Most book collectors are busy people, and they do not have the time to do all the homework, however interested in the subject they may be. So they ask a dealer whose knowledge and taste especially impresses them (or from whom they have bought regularly) to advise them. And since most auctions take place during working hours on weekdays it is often not possible for the collector to attend the auction himself. Thus it happens that the dealer receives a 'commission' from a collector to buy a certain lot at auction. The collector asks the dealer to view it for him, and to advise on the price the book is likely to fetch. When the dealer has done so, a maximum sum is decided on and later, at the sale, the dealer will bid on behalf of the collector. The transaction with the auctioneers is entirely in the dealer's name—his name is called out as the hammer falls, and he is responsible for paying the bill and for checking the book for his client. To the outside world, it is as though he has bought the lot for his own stock. So far as the dealer is concerned, a degree of trust must exist between himself and his customer, as he has spent money which he now has to recover. The customer often has also to trust the dealer, for the quality of the book's condition or appearance may be a matter of taste rather than fact, and the collector will frequently rely on the dealer's experience and opinions. So it is important, when commissioning a dealer to bid for you, to choose someone in whose judgement you have confidence.

Buying at auction need not always be done through a dealer, but at larger auctions or when buying expensive books it is advisable and all the major private collectors do so. They will use a dealer partly for privacy—conspicuous spending is nowadays less acceptable than in the past, and wider publicity is given to auctions—and partly for convenience. But most of all the collector will value having the dealer 'on his side' in the

Viewing before an auction at Christie's South Kensington, the sale room in London for items of lesser value. Lotting tickets identify the books in the printed catalogue, which is marked by viewers as they consider whether to bid on each lot. In the foreground is a box of mixed books, the proverbial 'job lot'.

auction: the dealer may have an eye to buying the book for his own stock, but he will sink his interests in those of his customer if he has been given a commission, and will act solely on his behalf. This occasionally has unfortunate results from the dealer's point of view, for he may buy on commission a book for which he would pay more if he were buying it for his own stock. If the bidding goes higher than his commission allows, he may of course buy the book for himself, but it will rarely be sensible to bid so much for stock.

What is the benefit to the dealer of buying on commission? Perhaps the most important advantage to him is publicity: buying good books at auction means that his name will become known to dealers and collectors alike (the name of his firm will be called out as he buys a lot, and it will appear in the published price-lists), and his reputation and turnover alike will increase. There is a financial inducement, too: a dealer will charge his customer 10 per cent on top of the price at which the hammer falls as a payment for his services. This will of course be a substantial sum if the lot costs thousands of pounds (although some negotiation on the percentage often takes place at the higher levels), but for the lower-priced lot a commission is not very productive for the dealer, and it is frequently almost a favour to the customer.

If you decide to bid for yourself at auction, a few simple rules should be learnt. There is an art to good bidding, but the mystique should be treated with scepticism: you will not suddenly find yourself the purchaser of an expensive lot simply because you scratched your nose at the wrong moment; nor, in most auction rooms, is there nowadays a 'ring' of dealers conspiring to keep out private buyers and defraud the seller. The techniques of bidding are simple and easily learnt, but they can be as easily forgotten in the excitement of an auction, and even experienced dealers will lose their judgement in the heat of the moment.

Before the auction begins the buyer should be clear in his mind as to how much he is prepared to pay for the lot in which he is interested—as clear as if he were asking someone else to bid for him. Of course, he may change his mind if the bidding on the sale is buoyant and prices are very high: auctions set prices in people's minds, and the buyer who does not

A recent book sale at Christie's, London. The auctioneer sees a bidder (bottom left, raising his pencil) and takes his bid. The porter beneath the auctioneer displays the book. At some book sales in London a table covered in green baize surrounds the area beneath the rostrum; in America this is absent.

adjust swiftly to what may be a new price-level can be left without the books at all. He should also view the book beforehand—most auctions will be on public view at least two days before the sale, and also on the morning of the sale itself. Except for large 'house sales' or exclusive sales of high-priced works of art, where a catalogue or a ticket may be required for entry, all auctions are open to the public, and may be attended by anyone with time and inclination. Most auctioneers now charge for their catalogues, and if you are not already a subscriber, you should buy one at the entrance, for it is on the description in the catalogue that the book will be sold.

Formal and courteous behaviour is the rule in an auction room—bidders do not yell or leap about. Bidding is usually conducted by a series of nods or discreet movements of the hand—or by a numbered paddle in some salerooms in America. Stand or sit towards the back of the room, so that you can observe the competition; if you draw attention to yourself you may encourage other bidders and so lose the book. When you want to join the bidding, the crucial step is to attract the notice of the auctioneer, who will not take your initial signal as a bid unless you are looking at him. Once the auctioneer knows that you are bidding, your signal need no longer be so demonstrative. Make your bids clear and regular, as anyone can become muddled if the bidding becomes fast, and bid only when the auctioneer looks back to you after taking the previous bid. It occasionally happens that a mix-up will result in a bid jumping up two stages at a time, but once the hammer has come down it may be too late to remedy the

situation. When you want to stop bidding, shake your head unmistakably: if you simply cease bidding, the auctioneer will probably understand quickly, but it is best to make your meaning clear.

The auctioneer will take the bids up in stages of roughly 10 per cent: for
instance, from 100 he will go up in tens, from 200 in twenties. But every
auctioneer has his own style and manner, some taking sales with agonizing
slowness, others moving with bewildering speed. So arrive in plenty of
time for the lots you want—most auctioneers sell at a rate of between two
and three lots per minute (120–180 per hour). This will allow you to get
the feel of the auction as it progresses, and to see what the competition is
likely to be. In auctions, more than in most things in the book trade,
experience tells, and when you have attended a few sales and got to know
some faces an auction becomes less intimidating and more enjoyable.

Once the hammer falls, and the lot is yours, you will become the legal
owner of the book you bid for. The amount you have to pay, however,
will not be simply the price at which the hammer fell: all the major auction
houses today charge a premium on top of the price you bid, to cover their
rising costs, and there may be additional taxes such as Value Added Tax
on the premium (in the United Kingdom) or sales tax (in many cities in the
United States). In Britain and North America the premiums vary from 8
per cent to 10 per cent; on the continent of Europe they are frequently
higher, usually 15 per cent and occasionally higher still. Make sure before
you bid that you have understood what additional charges you are liable
for—the conditions of sale will be stated in the catalogue.

Selling

No collector worth his or her salt goes through life without finding that
space, or economics, or changing interests dictate that some books must be
sold. It may seem gloomy to be looking so far ahead when the chase has
only just begun, but equally it may be a comfort to remember that you can
sell your books should the need arise. Who does not want to know that the
money he lays out is not being thrown away? Good books wisely bought
will appreciate in value—even good books foolishly bought do so, given
time. If you buy the books you understand and love, and buy prudently,
you will have the double satisfaction of owning them and knowing that
your money is invested well.

Nevertheless, it is essential to remember that you are unlikely to be able
to recoup your money immediately. Dealers in rare books, like dealers in
other articles which can be traded second-hand, cannot usually afford to
pay a higher price this year than they were asking last: when you buy a
book from a bookshop, you are paying not simply for the book but also for
the dealer to be there, to keep his shop open and to feed his children. So
you must view your collection as a long-term investment, rather than as a
commodity to be quickly traded at a fixed rate.

There are no rules for the disposing of a library. Some collectors will
treat only with one dealer; some like to sell to dealers other than those
from whom they bought. Many book-buyers feel that their books are
more likely to realize their best price at auction, where more than one

buyer will compete for them and where a public, or 'market', price can be struck. With large libraries, this obviously has an advantage, and many collectors have also felt a certain romantic attachment to the idea of seeing their books dispatched to the corners of the earth from the market-place. Edward Gibbon the historian was not the only one to have had such thoughts on the disposal of his library, but perhaps he put it better than most:

> 'I am a friend to the circulation of property of every kind, and besides the pecuniary advantage of my poor heirs, I consider a public sale as the most laudable method of disposing of it. From such sales my books were chiefly collected and when I can no longer use them they will again be culled by various buyers according to the measure of their wants and means.'

In recent years, because of a number of important sales and a string of high prices, the auction houses have come to dominate the scene. And in the dispersal of large libraries the auctioneer has always been at his best. However, for books of special interest and for the odd single book it may be worth your while to ask a dealer as well. He may be able to offer a good price, saving you the time and expense of offering it at auction. Touting the book around from dealer to dealer is not a good idea: a book can easily become too familiar and 'shop-soiled', especially if it subsequently appears in an auction. That said, auctions are unpredictable, and what may seem a fair price to one possible contender will be cheap to another — and many is the occasion on which a fair estimate in an auction catalogue has been doubled or trebled on the day.

Commission rates charged to the vendor vary, but most auction houses will take 10 per cent of the price at which the hammer falls, with slightly higher rates for cheaper lots. Many auction houses now provide an international service, and can sell your goods in a different city, or even a different country, if they feel the objects are likely to fetch a better price there. Their catalogues circulate all over the world, and are closely read by the major dealers; a few lots in the larger sale rooms will escape the attention of the best and most discriminating buyers. Clearly, with such a network covering the world of buyers and sellers, the auctioneers have a tremendous advantage over the dealers; but no-one in the trade is all-powerful or omniscient, and without these two competing halves of the book business there would be no business at all.

GOOD AND BAD TASTE

In the preceding pages the all-important question 'What is a good book?' has gone unanswered. No collector or dealer has a monopoly on good taste, and any attempt to lay down the law will always be hotly disputed; in any case our own ideas change as we grow older and wiser (or older and less wise). The following section will be concerned with obvious errors — errors of fact rather than errors of choice, since a collection of forgeries or imperfect books is hardly likely to be any collector's aim. The present section tries to enunciate certain basic standards of taste and discrimination. Sometimes these will seem like unattainable ideals, but they are not inflexible: if it were easy or cheap to find the best books in the best condition there would be no enjoyment in being a collector.

Standards also change according to the times. If you had been a moderately wealthy collector in London in the sixteenth century you could have bought books printed by Caxton which are now impossible to find—but at the time you might have been laughed at as a second-rate antiquary, for your contemporaries might have been buying Anglo-Saxon manuscripts, or the latest and finest continental books. Who on earth, they would have said, wants those out-of-date printed editions? And yet by the middle of the eighteenth century, when the fashion for collecting early printing was just beginning, the same antiquated volumes were being sought by collectors in every corner of every library.

Similarly, fashions which gripped a generation of collectors as recently as fifty years ago now leave their successors coldly unenthusiastic. If, for example, you bought great works of eighteenth-century English literature from the most expensive American dealers in the 1930s, the cost was likely to be exorbitant even by today's standards. One American collector, Marjorie Wiggin Prescott, bought two novels by Tobias Smollett at $1,500 and $1,000 in 1930; when her books were sold at auction in 1981 after her death, bidders were prepared to pay only $320 and $100 for them. High fashion, like a high tide, will always leave some melancholy sights on the beaches of time.

But the story is by no means always so gloomy, and even Mrs Prescott's costly collection showed a handsome profit in many areas. It is unrealistic to suppose that fashions will not change, and that those changes will leave prices unaffected. In a comparatively short space of time, competition among a group of collectors pursuing the same sort of books can raise prices dramatically and permanently. Nothing is more instructive—and frustrating—in this instance than to look through booksellers' catalogues of a previous generation and imagine that the books were still available at the prices then quoted. Since the Second World War, of course, the prices for all antiques and works of art have risen spectacularly as the fashion for collecting has spread and disposable income has increased. But it is still scarcely believable that in the 1950s fine and highly desirable books could be bought for what now seem ludicrously low prices. The firm of William H. Robinson, then one of the grandest and most expensive booksellers in London, in 1950 offered a Greek manuscript of the Gospels, written in Constantinople in 1271, for a mere £325. From the same catalogue you might have bought a fine copy of the first book on logarithms (John Napier's *Mirifici logarithmorum canonis descriptio*, 1614) for £250, or James I of England's own copy of his poetical works for £600. These are all books which now seem to have been almost given away, but at the time the prices must have seemed steep. Had you bought these books then, you would find that their value had shot up by perhaps 20 to 30 times between then and now—considerably above the rate of inflation—and no doubt their owners today are well pleased with their foresight.

Claude-Joseph Dorat, *Fables nouvelles*, 2 volumes, Paris, 1773.

The delicate engravings by French eighteenth-century artists show the harmony of illustration and the printed book. Often treated as decadent or fanciful by English and American collectors, the best-decorated books of this time command high prices from French collectors, provided the book is in fine condition.

Collectors should always seek books in their original bindings. *Scenes of Clerical Life* was the first work of fiction by George Eliot, and it had a small sale. Copies in the original cloth in such fine conditions are rare and desirable.

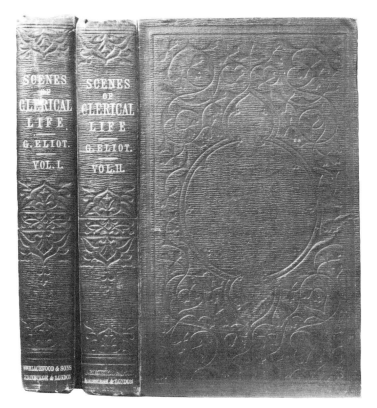

Why have their books appreciated so much, when Mrs Prescott's fifty-year 'investment' in two Smollett novels showed such losses? It is not really surprising that some not particularly rare novels in shabby condition, bought at the top end of a boom market, should have shown a dismal loss. It is equally clear that an important book such as Napier's *Logarithms*—the basis of logarithmic mathematics—is going to rise in price as copies disappear into institutional libraries and as enthusiasts of the history of science develop their collections. To detail the reasons for these differing fates is not easy, but it may help the new collector if we talk in terms of three guiding principles: rarity, importance and interest, and condition.

Rarity

The rarity of most printed books is relative. Some books are absolutely rare, surviving in their original editions in no more than two or three copies. Others are now so rare outside institutional libraries that they are rare from the collector's point of view: they are rare, that is, on the open market. A book may never be seen in a bookseller's stock and yet be present in four copies in the British Library and in two or three at one of the great American university libraries such as Harvard or Yale. In fact, the presence of more than one copy of a book in libraries such as these suggests to the wise bookman that some especial interest attaches to it, for copies will have been bequeathed by collectors of taste and discrimination. As one wise but eccentric bookseller used to say: 'If the British Library has three copies of a book, it *must* be rare.'

Does a book then have quality because it is hard to find? Not necessarily so. Many books are rare in one way or another; the collector's object is to collect those books which are both hard to find and interesting because of their content or condition. The umpteenth edition of Euclid's geometry may be an uncommon book—but unless the edition has some intrinsic interest other than its rarity no collector is likely to give it a second glance. The first edition of Euclid, by contrast, printed in Venice in 1483, is (by the standards of such books) not difficult to find for sale—yet because it is the *first* edition of so fundamental a work, and also because that particular edition is a handsome book in its own right, the price will always be very high.

The scarcity of any book, or of any type of book, is something which can be gauged in a number of ways, but the best point of reference is experience: how many times have I seen that book (or one like it) for sale before? Various standard works of reference (see pp.152–5) list the known copies of books of a certain type or period. But they should be treated with caution, since even the most thorough reference work cannot list *all* known copies, and some books will be commoner than the work suggests. With experience you will come to know the strengths and shortcomings of particular works, and the likely rarity of certain types of book.

A few rules, which must be taken only as rules of thumb, can be suggested concerning the survival of books. These are:

1. Small books are less likely to survive than big books: folio or other large-format books would have been expensive when printed and they will have been kept with greater care than smaller, less grand, editions.

2. Books that were expensively produced will be preserved when low-priced books are destroyed. This is an extension of the previous point: a book which cost the original owner dear will attract care from his successors.

3. Books produced for children are much less likely to survive than books for adults.

4. Newspapers, pamphlets, sensational reports and other ephemera—generally sold in the street to passers-by and discarded when read—will always be uncommon. Because so many of them were printed they are not rare as a *genre*, and plenty of examples can usually be found; but of any particular copy not more than a very few are likely to survive.

5. Books by authors obscure or unknown to their contemporaries are likely to be rare, not because they were thrown away by their original purchasers but because the printer or publisher would probably not have risked a large print-run.

Importance and interest

What makes a book interesting to the collector in the first place? The bible that Johann Gutenberg printed in about 1450–5, the first printed book,

A few copies of the finer books of the eighteenth and nineteenth centuries were sometimes printed on specially large sheets of paper, so that the finished product had wide margins. These are known as 'large paper copies'. The refinement was taken to extremes by some printers at the end of the eighteenth century when enormous sheets were used for quite small pages of type, giving margins that were luxuriously and absurdly large.

remains pre-eminent among books which changed the way we see the world. The significance of many other books may not be so clear, and their importance is often greater to us today than it would have been to contemporaries—which is why modern booksellers and collectors sometimes attach an iconic significance to books which contain the first appearance in print of, say, a poem, or a discovery.

Book collectors are often teased by their friends for spending what appear to be disproportionate sums of money on books whose texts could be purchased for small change. The collector can happily agree that it would indeed be ridiculous to buy a book for a hundred pounds if all he wanted to do with it was to read it. If you want only to read Keats's *Endymion* you can borrow a copy from a friend: but to possess the first edition, and to see it as Keats's first readers would have seen it, places a different emphasis on the act of reading the poem. Thus the earliest editions of any book which has a particular importance for the collector himself will automatically become a candidate for his library.

The search for the first edition of a book has a solid basis of sense for the collector, since not only does it bring him closest to the author's age and to the text as he wrote it, but the first edition is always likely to be the hardest to find. If you were a collector of Dante, for instance, your final goal would be to own a copy of the first edition of the *Divine Comedy*, published at Foligno in 1472; but because the book is both rare and expensive you might have to approach it through the sixteenth-century editions, many of which are both interesting and relatively cheap, and then move back into the fifteenth century. This would give you an interesting perspective on the way that readers thought of Dante over a hundred years or more.

The interest of a printed book need not only be in its text. A strikingly different approach, current especially amongst French collectors, is to buy not the earliest but the 'best' edition. In this context 'the best' is judged by the quality of the printing and illustration. Of La Fontaine's *Fables*, one of the most frequently reprinted of all French literary texts, the best edition is therefore not the first (1668) but one of four folio volumes published in 1755–9, with magnificent engravings after designs by Jean-Baptiste Oudry. Although this is a much commoner book than the first edition, a good copy in a fine contemporary morocco binding will excite strong competition among collectors. Fine printing from private presses— principally an interest pursued in the English-speaking world—can be another basis for a collection. The explosion of private press production in the twentieth century means that the work of many lesser presses is available at prices within everyone's reach—from £20 upwards— whether buying straight from the printer or second-hand.

These are all ways in which the collector can vary his approach to the formation of a library and we will be discussing them in greater detail in the second part of this book (pp.53–113). Here we are concerned with showing that the collector should be collecting books for the sake of their intrinsic interest, not merely because they are rare or because of their fine binding: there must be a conjunction of the physical quality of the book— its scarcity or its good condition—with some higher and more conceptual aim.

A word must be added about 'association' copies. One of the most rewarding ways of collecting books is to look especially for interesting associations between the book and its owner. Thus a copy of Dickens's *A Tale of Two Cities* (1859) with an inscription on the title-page by Dickens presenting the book to George Eliot 'with high admiration and regard' (such a copy was actually sold at auction a few years ago) is one of the most desirable copies one could imagine, potent as it is with interest for the student of both Dickens and George Eliot. A similar copy given by Dickens to someone of less interest would be correspondingly less

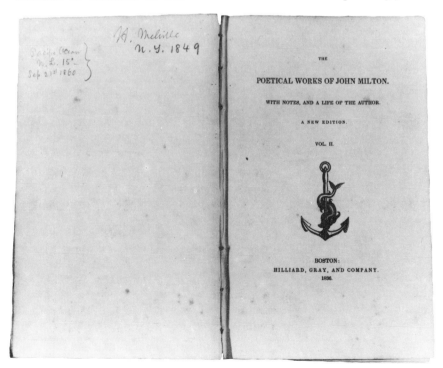

An association copy of rare importance. Herman Melville was much influenced by Milton in writing his masterpiece, *Moby Dick*. His annotated copy of the poet's works appeared at auction in New York in 1984 and reached the sensational price of $110,000 (£80,000). Less glamorous associations command more manageable prices.

Avoid mutilated or defaced copies: not only does this book have its title page defaced with a large library stamp, but someone has cut away the foot of the page, doubtless to get rid of the signature of a former owner.

collectable. Few association copies, indeed, can be so glamorous as this, and they need not all be of such critical interest. Such admittedly minor sidelights on the history of a book can nevertheless form the basis for a striking collection, since an association copy is set apart from all copies by the history of its ownership. Moreover, as some famous owners' marks are obscure and their connection with the work perhaps recondite there is ample opportunity for original discoveries to be made.

Condition

The condition in which a book is found will be of considerable importance in determining its quality and value. With some rare and significant books *any* copy, even a poor or incomplete one, may be worth buying: who knows when you may see another? But generally the rule must always be to buy books only in the best condition. Not everyone can be rich or patient enough to follow this advice to the letter, but as you see more books and your taste grows more sophisticated you may well find that your definition of acceptable quality narrows. The most important rules to bear in mind, which again are adaptable to circumstances, are:

1. Always make sure that a book is 'perfect'—booksellers' jargon for complete—since an imperfect book is frowned upon by collectors. Modern taste perhaps places too much emphasis on a book's being perfect: some parts of a book, such as their half-title or appended publisher's advertisements, were often regarded by contemporaries as unnecessary and were discarded before the book was bound.

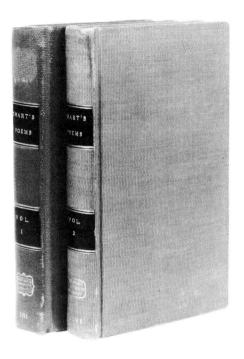

2. Always try to find books in their original condition. For some books there are two ways of approaching this point: some collectors seek books in their original state—that is, as they were when they emerged from the printer's shop. These are books 'in boards', untouched by the binder (see below, pp.131–2). But the practice of covering books in temporary bindings represents a relatively short—though highly significant—period in the history of the book. With the evolution of cloth bindings in the nineteenth century, publishers and book buyers came to regard the binding in which the book was issued as its permanent covering. An original cloth binding should therefore be regarded as an integral part of the book, and whilst a contemporary calf or morocco binding on an eighteenth-century book may be regarded as the 'original' covering, this is not true of most English and American books from the 1830s on.

3. Do not buy books which have unpleasant marks such as foxing (brown spots and stains caused by chemicals originally present in the paper) or other unsightly stains. Some books, though, were made with such bad paper that copies are nearly always foxed, so a lower standard has to be adopted.

4. Avoid books which have been heavily restored, especially if the restoration is inexpert. Books in which the paper has deteriorated are sometimes treated by having the leaves washed and 'resized' (the paper treated with chemicals as it was when originally made). Conspicuous repairs to the paper of a book are also to be shunned.

ABOVE LEFT
Books which have been re-bound in an inappropriate style should be shunned: this copy of Smart's *Poems* (1791) was stoutly covered for library use some time this century but was later sold as a duplicate. Such a book should be sought in a calf or morocco binding.

ABOVE
Foxing and other stains give a book a nasty appearance. In books printed on a bad stock of paper this may be unavoidable, but some copies will have been better preserved than others.

5. Booksellers sometimes take imperfect copies of books and insert the missing leaves from another copy: this is, on the whole, not a good practice and is not much indulged in nowadays. It can easily be detected if the inserted leaf is shorter or narrower than the other leaves, or if it has stains which mark it out from its immediate surroundings.

As before, these can only be notes to guide the collector, and no advice can be a substitute for experience. But it is essential that sound principles be learnt from the beginning, even if they have to be modified in practice.

We are perhaps no nearer the answer to the question 'What is a good book?' than at the beginning of this section. But, in effect, there can be only one answer: it is the book which interests and excites *you*. If others share your enthusiasm the competition is likely to be stiffer—but you will have the consolation of the chase being more enjoyable and the final rewards greater.

PITFALLS

This appears to be a little booklet of poems published by Marian Lewes (the married name of 'George Eliot') in 1869. It is actually a forgery printed after 1880, probably for T. J. Wise, who sold copies of this and other forgeries for considerable sums up until the 1930s.

BROTHER AND SISTER

SONNETS

BY

MARIAN LEWES

LONDON

FOR PRIVATE CIRCULATION ONLY

1869

'The whole thing proves once more that, easy as it appears to be to fabricate reprints of rare books, it is in actual practice absolutely impossible to do so in such a manner that detection cannot follow the result.' With this authoritative judgement by Thomas James Wise, veteran book collector and past president of the Bibliographical Society of London, John Carter and Graham Pollard opened *An Enquiry into the Nature of Certain Nineteenth Century Pamphlets* (1934). The solemnly descriptive title masked the explosive nature of the contents, and the revelations of their 'Enquiry' were to become the greatest scandal to hit the book world for decades. For what Carter and Pollard revealed, by an elaborate process of scientific detection, was that a number of apparently very rare literary pamphlets of the later nineteenth century—mostly purporting to be private editions specially commissioned by their authors—were forgeries printed considerably later and without authorial licence: forgeries executed by deception and sold for gain. Fearful of libel, the authors were unable to call the criminal publicly to account, but the finger of suspicion throughout the book points unmistakably at that pillar of respectability whose opinion on bibliographical forgery stands as an ironical epigraph to the work, Thomas J. Wise himself.

Wise died in 1937, maintaining a Trappist silence on the whole matter, but his career as a forger, which has become still clearer over the years, offers both a fascinating story and a cautionary tale. In practice it is indeed nearly impossible to forge a book: simple comparison with another copy will reveal some disparity, however small. Wise, however, acted with considerable ingenuity in forging (almost exclusively) books which could have existed, but which were not known: so how could the bibliographer compare them with other copies? In this way a large number (nearly 100 at the latest count) of small books with false dates, all by famous Victorian authors—Dickens, Tennyson, Ruskin, the two Brownings, George Eliot and many others—were fed onto the antiquarian book market, confusing

PUBLII VIRGILII

MARONIS

BUCOLICA,

GEORGICA,

ET

AENEIS.

BIRMINGHAMIAE:

Typis JOHANNIS BASKERVILLE.

MDCCLVII.

This looks like the first edition of Baskerville's famous *Virgil*, 1757. In fact it is a very precise reprint, made probably by Baskerville himself some years later: the position of the printer's name is slightly to the left in this printing, distinguishing it from the 'real' Baskerville *Virgil*.

the collector, scholar and librarian alike. New research methods, and a painstaking analysis of letter-forms—certain letter-forms were not available at the time of the supposed printing—allowed Carter and Pollard to reveal that most of the books were printed during the 1890s or later, and that the ultimate source of many of them could not be traced beyond the collections of Wise himself, or of his collaborator, Harry Buxton Forman.

The tale of T. J. Wise is instructive in several ways: most importantly, it shows how even elaborate precautions fail to conceal a forgery from scientific detection. But it also shows how important the element of trust and honesty is in bookdealing. A number of collectors had paid high prices for Wise's products, and whilst one can be confident that a crime will always meet its Sherlock Holmes in the end, it may by then be too late to recover your money. The bookdealer and scholar alike know, therefore, that they cannot afford to wink at such malpractices, since the trust of customers and readers is vital.

None the less, forgeries and fakes of one sort or another can slip through, and not all of them begin with an attempt to deceive. If you have an eighteenth-century book in a binding beyond repair, it is good sense to have it re-bound in a style appropriate to the period. It is not then your fault—or that of the binder—if a subsequent owner mistakes it for a contemporary binding. Collectors who have bought imperfect books (because complete copies would have been either unobtainable or beyond their means) may choose to have photolithographic facsimiles bound in. And if they are fastidious they will want their replacement to resemble the original as closely as possible, using old paper and binding the new leaf in with the old so that the book looks complete. These practices are not intended criminally or morally to deceive, but an unwitting collector after the event may still lay out his money mistakenly.

By education or experience most collectors eventually come to recognize obvious forgeries. The essential preparation is a knowledge of what a book from the period should look like: would a binder in 1750 have used leather like this? Or could this type of paper have been used in 1880? Experts in detection have more closely defined questions to ask and tests to run, but we give below a few of the most important points to look out for.

Printed Matter

Facsimile leaves in a book are perhaps the most common form of deception that you may encounter, since forging whole books is virtually impossible (and, where tried, well documented). Single leaves are usually fairly easy to detect, since the whole of the rest of the book will stand as a witness to what the leaf should look like. Inserted facsimile leaves are rarer in modern books, which of course are less likely to have been re-bound or otherwise altered from their original form, and are therefore almost always above suspicion. The present cautions apply mostly to books printed before 1800, where long use or neglect may have resulted in the loss of a leaf—usually at the beginning or end of the book, but in practice at any point. Here you should watch out for:

1. Paper which does not match the rest of the book. Is the paper 'laid'— that is, do you see wide stripes one way and narrow the other when you hold it to the light; or is it 'wove', where the frame on which the paper was made created a homogeneous texture? Wove paper is a relatively modern invention: it was not manufactured until the 1750s, and does not appear with any regularity until the 1770s. So if the book is any earlier a leaf of wove paper is certainly a later addition. Watch out also for the watermark itself: if it does not match the other leaves, your suspicions should be aroused. And if the paper seems in any way thicker, thinner, or a different colour from the rest, check if this is so with the leaves which constitute the rest of the sheet (see pp.121–4).

2. Ink of a different colour or texture. Occasionally a slightly greyer colour to the ink, and a smoother texture to the paper, may mean that the leaf is genuine but has been washed and resized to remove stains. But often it will mean that the matching of the ink in making the facsimile has not been good enough.

3. Edges of the paper which fail to match the rest of the book. If the leaf is genuine, it may nevertheless have been inserted from another copy.

When the edges of the book are gilt or otherwise decorated, it is difficult to match the edges precisely and a slight difference may give the game away.

4. Type which does not match. This rather obvious point ought to be noted none the less. Occasionally a missing leaf can be imitated using old type, but the two alphabets will never be exactly the same; and painstaking facsimile-makers have been known to produce facsimiles by hand, closely imitating the print with their pens.

It should be emphasized that the manufacture of facsimile leaves is hardly practised nowadays, and that the best facsimiles, being expensive, will be found only in the most expensive books—the sort of book which in any case the dealer and auctioneer will take the greatest care in describing. Only one book in a thousand will need or be worth making a facsimile for, and only one in ten thousand will have been given one.

Which is the facsimile? The page on the right has been photocopied onto old paper, with the result that slight marks in the original have shown up in an unnatural black similar to the type. Examination of the actual book would also show that the paper, although similar to the rest of the book, is slightly different in texture, and that the ink is blacker than an original.

Bindings

Imitation or 'pastiche' bindings are more common than facsimile leaves, but they are less difficult to spot than a good facsimile. The recent growth

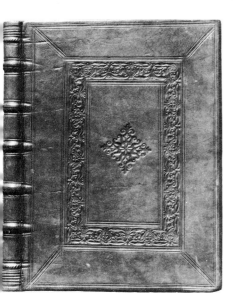

This modern binding on a book of 1521 attempts to reproduce—although not to forge—the sort of binding that might once have covered it: brown calfskin, blind tooled in an imprecise manner in a characteristic panelled pattern.

in the study of binding history has exposed the weakness of previous imitations, and has simultaneously encouraged more sophisticated attempts; in practice, though, it is next to impossible to forge an old leather binding. Any imitation of an old binding executed before the middle of this century is likely to be either the work of an old-fashioned binder who is unconsciously using a traditional style, or a binding inspired by old designs and not intended to deceive. A new or recent binding will generally look new, and not even the cleverest imitators have succeeded in ageing their bindings more than a little. Some genuine old bindings, of course, survive in miraculously good condition, looking as if they have just come from the binder's shop: experience alone can tell you which are later work, and which the real thing. Two important points remain to be made:

1. Books in boards. Books issued by the publisher in the later eighteenth and early nineteenth centuries were often in rudimentary bindings known as boards—that is, pasteboard covers with paper spines, often with printed paper labels pasted to the spines. It is possible to re-create such a style of binding nearly exactly, but printing labels to match is extremely difficult: they will inevitably look wrong. Be wary of a book in boards in brilliant condition—almost all authentic bindings will have deteriorated to some extent—and of a book which does not have printed labels (although labels were not always issued). Fakes can often be determined by examining the endpapers: they should be consistent with the paper in the rest of the book. If they fail this test, the whole binding may well be an imitation.

2. Binders' tickets. In France during the later eighteenth century the craft of binding gained great prestige, and certain binders began to 'sign' their bindings with small printed labels pasted inside the covers. This practice was imitated by workmen in England, many of them German émigrés, around the beginning of the nineteenth century, and later binders took to 'signing' their bindings by tooling their names discreetly on the dentelles. The printed paper labels were easily removable, and as the bindings of the French binder Derome and a few others were vastly more valuable than most, it was tempting for dishonest dealers to remove Derome's label from a binding that had deteriorated and paste it into an anonymous binding in better condition. This sort of deception, however, is extremely uncommon and will usually occur only with French bindings of the eighteenth century—an area which is in any case full of problems for the uninitiated.

Manuscripts

This book does not pretend to deal with the collecting of manuscripts, except insofar as it strays into traditional book collecting areas, so only a few words need be said on this enormous subject. The forging of manuscripts for gain has been practised for many centuries, but recent developments in technique have made the detection of forgeries much easier. Almost every great historical or literary figure has had forged documents assigned to his or her hand, from Jesus to Hitler. Forgery for

MISCELLANEOUS PAPERS

AND

LEGAL INSTRUMENTS

UNDER THE HAND AND SEAL OF

WILLIAM SHAKSPEARE:

INCLUDING THE TRAGEDY

OF

KING LEAR,

AND A SMALL FRAGMENT

OF

HAMLET,

FROM THE ORIGINAL MSS.

IN THE POSSESSION OF

SAMUEL IRELAND,

OF NORFOLK STREET.

——" Quod optanti Divum promittere nemo."
" Auderet, volvenda dies en attulit ultro."
Æn. IX. 6.

London:

Printed by Cooper and Graham, Bow Street, Covent Garden.
Published by Mr. Egerton, Whitehall; Messrs. White, Fleet
Street ; Messrs. Leigh and Sotheby, York Street, Covent
Garden ; Mr. Robson, and Mr. Faulder, New Bond Street;
and Mr. Sael, opposite St. Clement's Church.

1796.

resale is a comparatively modern phenomenon: the most common attempts tend to be made on the writings of literary figures of the eighteenth and nineteenth centuries (being closest to the forgers' own times), but forgeries of earlier figures were regularly made in the nineteenth century, the favourite in the English-speaking world being of course William Shakespeare. In fact, so frequently were signatures or whole manuscripts put forward as the work of his hand during the nineteenth century, that a wall of disbelief would greet the genuine article in the twentieth. And the forgeries themselves, like the printed forgeries of Wise and Forman, are much sought after by collectors of such historical impedimenta.

However, several forgeries of more modern figures (most of them done in the nineteenth century) still circulate on the market; even when recognized they have no natural home, and some old chestnuts turn up again and again, discovered by one person only to be exposed by another. The list of names whose hands have been forged is perhaps predictable, and it includes authors whose manuscripts are common (and therefore to be expected on the market) as well as authors whose manuscripts are very rare (and therefore highly saleable). Forgeries of Burns, Byron, Shelley—though not, for some reason, Keats—Charlotte Brontë and Oscar Wilde are the ones most likely to be encountered. Romantic figures such as Nelson or

William Henry Ireland, *Miscellaneous Papers and Legal Instruments under the Hand and Seal of William Shakespeare*, London, 1796.

W. H. Ireland's forgeries of Shakespeare's hand fooled most people in London in the 1790s, including his father Samuel. Today they seem very crude, and books relating to them are collected for their interest as the first successful Shakespeare fraud.

Collecting medieval miniatures is closely allied to book collecting. One trap to watch out for is the work of 'The Spanish Forger', a skilful artist who imitated medieval paintings with some success at the beginning of this century. Even now his identity is unknown, but his work is collected for its own interest: this painting fetched £385 ($925) when it was sold at auction in 1980.

Napoleon, or important American statesmen such as Washington or Lincoln, may also be targets for the forger. The principal reason for these forgeries is their popularity with unwary collectors who have no specialist knowledge and no experts to call upon.

These cautionary notes may have made you unnecessarily sceptical, and you may think that a forgery awaits you at every turn. This is not so: you will be unfortunate if you buy even one 'bad' book or manuscript from a dealer. But on tricky matters it is always best to go to a major dealer or auctioneer—their homework will usually be sounder, and their reputation the greater to lose—or to a large public library or university research library, where the staff will be able to provide an unbiased opinion based on proven documents in their collections. A conspiracy of honesty and expertise in the trade, among dealers and auctioneers alike, has made it very difficult in recent years for forgeries of any sort to escape unnoticed. The very business depends on trust and on the maintenance of that trust, and every bookseller and auctioneer would rather sell no books at all than pass on fakes to their customers.

Incipit liber bresith quē nos genesim
dr principio creauit deus celū dicim⁹
et terram. Terra autem erat inanis et
vacua: et tenebre erāt sup faciē abissi.
et sps dūi ferebāt sup aquas. Dixitqz
deus. fiat lux. Et facta ē lux. Et vidit
deus lucem cp esset bona: z diuisit lucē
a tenebris. appellauitqz lucem diem z
tenebras noctem. factūqz est vespe et
mane dies vnus. Dixit qz deus. fiat
firmamentū in medio aquarz: z diui-
dat aquas ab aquis. Et fecit deus firmamentū: diuisitqz aquas que erāt
sub firmamento ab hijs qz erant sup
firmamentū. et factū ē ita. Vocauitqz
deus firmamentū celū: z factū ē vespe
et mane dies secūd⁹. Dixit vero deus.
Congregent aque que sub celo sūt in
locū vnū z appareat arida. Et factū ē
ita. Et vocauit deus aridam terram:
congregacionesqz aquarz appellauit
maria. Et vidit deus cp esset bonū. et
ait. Germinet terra herbā virentem et
facientē semen: z lignū pomiferz faciēs
fructū iuxta genus suū: cui⁹ semen in
semetipso sit sup terrā. Et factū ē ita. Et
protulit terra herbā virentē z facientē
semē iuxta genus suū: lignūqz faciēs
fructū z habes vnūqdqz sementē secdm
speciē suā. Et vidit deus cp esset bonū:
et factū est vespe et mane dies tercius.
Dixitqz autē deus. fiant luminaria
in firmamēto celi: z diuidāt diem ac
noctem: z sint in signa z tpa et dies z
annos. ut luceāt in firmamēto celi et
illuminēt terrā. Et factū ē ita. fecit
deus duo luminaria magna: lumiare
maius ut pesset diei et lumiare min⁹
ut pesset nocti z stellas. z posuit eas in
firmamēto celi ut lucerēt sup terrā: et

pessent diei ac nocti. z diuiderent lucē
ac tenebras. Et vidit de⁹ cp esset bonū:
et factū ē vespe z mane dies quartus.
Dixit eciā de⁹. Producāt aque reptile
anime viuentis z volatile super terrā
sub firmamēto celi. Creauitqz deus cete
grandia. et omnē aiam viuentē atqz
motabilē quā pduxerāt aque i species
suas. z omne volatile secdm gen⁹ suū.
Et vidit deus cp esset bonū. benedixitqz
eis dicens. Crescite z mltiplicamini. z
replete aquas maris. auesqz mltipli-
cēt sup terrā. Et factū ē vespe z mane
dies quitus. Dixit quoqz deus. Pro-
ducat terra aiam viuentē in genē suo
iumenta z reptilia. z bestias terre secdm
species suas. factūqz ē ita. Et fecit de⁹
bestias terre iuxta species suas. iumenta z omne reptile terre i genere suo. Et
vidit deus cp esset bonū. et ait. facia-
mus hoiem ad ymaginē z similitudinē
nostrā. z presit piscibz maris. et volatilibz celi z bestijs vniuersisqz terre. omniqz
repfili qd mouetur i terra. Et creauit
deus hoiem ad ymaginē z similitudinē
suā. ad ymaginē dei creauit illū. ma-
sculū z feminā creauit eos. Benedixit
qz illis deus. z ait. Crescite z mltiplicamini z replete terrā. et sbicite eā. et dūa-
mini piscibz maris. et volatilibz celi
et vniuersis animātibz que mouent
sup terrā. Dixitqz de⁹. Ecce dedi vobis
omnē herbā afferentē semen sup terrā
et vniūsa ligna que hūt in semetipis
sementē genis sui. ut sint vobis i escā
z cundis aiantibz terre. omniqz volucri
celi z vniuersis qz mouētur in terra. z i
quibz est anima viuēs. ut habeāt ad
vescendū. Et factū est ita. Viditqz deus
cuncta que fecerat. z erāt valde bona.

2. Tastes and Trends in Book Collecting

EARLY PRINTERS AND FINE PRINTING

The Invention of Printing

The art of printing is a technique of great antiquity: centuries before it was perfected in the West, Korean and Chinese inventors had found that by engraving shapes on blocks of wood they could print characters and reproduce them in quantity. Europeans in the mid-fifteenth century also developed such a system, using it to print primitive books, with the words and pictures cut into a single block of wood for each page. These books, of which only a very few survive today, are generally known as 'block books', and the technical term for the printing method is 'xylographic printing'.

The technique of printing with movable type was invented at about the same date by Johann Gutenberg, a goldsmith born in the German city of Mainz about the year 1400. Gutenberg's method did not replace the block book, which never developed as a useful instrument of communication (and whose invention may not even pre-date his own technique). His method of printing was perfected as a rival to and eventually as a replacement for manuscript copies of texts. Printing also hugely expanded the readership for all literature, sacred and secular; it made possible a wide increase in learning, and the rapid progress of civilization to which that gave birth.

Gutenberg's place in history is not as the 'inventor of printing'. What he did invent was the technique of printing with individually cast interchangeable metal types (a type is a single letter form): this double insight was to dominate printing for three hundred years. The first advantage of this was that the types could be infinitely rearranged to reproduce any text; the second was that by casting the letters in metal from a matrix the letters could be reproduced in quantity. With these two advances, printing needed no significant further technical development to be the powerful instrument it rapidly became.

But Gutenberg must have had many smaller practical difficulties, and it is astonishing that his first complete printed book, a Bible finished about

Biblia Latina, Mainz, Johann Gutenberg, c.1450–5.

The first leaf of Genesis in a copy of the Gutenberg Bible shows how marginal decoration was added in by hand in most copies, giving them the appearance of a manuscript. It was some years before books acquired characteristics of design which distinguished them radically from illuminated manuscripts.

1455 (now generally known as the 'Gutenberg Bible') remains in many ways the greatest of all printed books for the beauty of its execution and the surefooted mastery of the printer. Nearly fifty copies (some now incomplete) survive today: all of these are now in institutional libraries and are unlikely to be sold, although as recently as 1978 one was sold at Christie's New York for $2,200,000. Such books are not, of course, within the reach of private collectors; but single leaves from an incomplete copy that was split up this century have recently sold at auction for prices within the $5,000–7,000 range.

Incunabula

Books printed in the fifteenth century are known as 'incunabula', a Latin word meaning 'things from the cradle'. Not all incunabula are expensive: minor examples can be obtained for as little as £250, and incomplete copies for less, though rare and fine editions sell for very high prices. Many great collections have concentrated on such early books, illustrating the spread of printing throughout Europe—to Italy in 1465; to France in 1470; to the Netherlands in 1472; and to London in 1476, brought by William Caxton, an English merchant in the Low Countries.

The earliest printed books from any country are naturally a focal point for modern collectors of that nation, and Caxton's work now fetches particularly high prices in relation to his international significance (which is not great) because his books have remained attractive first to English and then to American collectors. The artistic quality of Caxton's books is low, even in comparison with his contemporaries: the design reflects the

ABOVE, LEFT

Hartmann Schedel, *Liber Cronicarum*, Nuremberg, Anton Koberger, 1493.

The 'Nuremberg Chronicle', as Schedel's book is known, has a fine series of woodcut views of cities. Woodcuts were expensive, however, and the views of Toulouse and Milan, shown here, feature elsewhere as pictures of cities as various as Pisa, Tiberias, Lacedaemon and Troyes.

ABOVE

John Gower, *Confessio Amantis*, Westminster, William Caxton, 1483.

The first edition of Gower's long moral poem. Lacking some of its leaves, like nearly all copies of Caxton's books on the market, this copy made £24,200 ($47,190) at auction in 1981.

Devices of famous early printers: (a) Johann Fust and Peter Schoeffer, successors to Gutenberg at Mainz; (b) the anchor and dolphin of Aldus Manutius at Venice; (c) William Caxton's bold initials, used also by his successor in London, Wynkyn de Worde; (d) the device of the Estienne family, printers in Paris, Geneva and elsewhere in the sixteenth and seventeenth centuries; (e) the compasses of Christopher Plantin, the prolific printer of Antwerp, with his motto 'Labor et scientia' (industry and knowledge).

provincial nature of English culture at the time, when the fresh wind of the Continental Renaissance had hardly wafted across the Channel. Copies of his books, and those of his successor, a German named Wynkyn de Worde, are mostly in great libraries: of Caxton's books, however, single leaves are sometimes sold at auction for £250 and upwards; books printed by de Worde are commoner but none the less expensive, depending upon the interest of the text.

By 1500 over twenty thousand different editions of books had been printed throughout Europe; so the range for the collector is wide, from the large number of early bibles to works of popular literature, from grand illustrated books such as Hartmann Schedel's *Liber Cronicarum* ('Book of Chronicles', known as the 'Nuremberg Chronicle', 1493) to little school-books such as that of the grammarian Donatus, frequently reprinted and now very rare. If some of the productions of fifteenth-century presses seem to the new collector extremely expensive, the prices should perhaps be compared with those for other artefacts of the same period: furniture, textiles and paintings of a similar age all cost many times the average price of a fifteenth-century book.

Fine Printing through the Ages

The development of printing in England was a slow process, greatly hampered by a governmental censorship which restricted the number of printers and fiercely controlled their output: not until the seventeenth century did the printing press in London come to realize its potential; and then it was as a means of communication and polemic, rather than as a medium for the creation of art. So it is to the continent of Europe, and in particular to Italy, that we must turn for the development of fine printing in its early stages.

The artistic world in Italy around the year 1500 was the milieu which bred Leonardo, Michelangelo and Titian. To the historian of printing it is the names of Nicolas Jenson (a Frenchman who printed in Venice), Aldo Manuzio (Aldus Manutius in the latinized form of his name) and the Giunta family which command admiration. A double debt is owed to these

to optatissime carne sentendo , nelle quale lalma sua uigendo, se nutri=
ua se euigiloe suspirulante, & reaperte le occlule palpebre . Et io repente
auidissima anhellando alla sua insperata reiteratione riceuute le debilita=
te & abandonate bracce, piamente, & cum dulcissime & amorose lachry=
mule cum singultato pertractantilo, & manuagendulo, & souente basian
tilo, præsentandogli, gli monstraua il mio, Immo suo albente & pomige=
ro pecto palesemente, cum humanissimo aspecto, & cum illici ochii esso
sécia uario di hora, riuéne nelle mie caste & delicate bracce, Quale si læsio
ne patito non hauesse, & alquantulo reassumete il contaminato uigore,
Como alhora ello ualeua, cum tremula uoce, & suspiritti , mansuetamen
tedisse, Polia Signora mia dolce, perche cusi atorto me fai? Di subito, O
me Nymphe celeberrime, me sentiui quasi de dolcecia amorosa, & pieto=
sa & excessiua alacritate il core p medio piu molto dilacerare, per che quel
sangue che per dolore, & nimia formidine in se era constricto p troppo &
inusitata læticia, laxare le uene il sentiua exhausto, & tuta absorta, & attoni
ta ignoraua che me dire, Si non che io agli ancora pallidati labri, cum so=
luta audacia, gli offersi blandicula uno lasciuo & mustulento basio, Am=
bi dui serati, & constrecti in amorosi amplexi, Quali nel Hermetico Ca=
duceo gli intrichatamente conuoluti serpi, & quale il baculo inuoluto
del diuino Medico.

men: not only were they printing for the first time the works of many
important classical authors—to Aldus alone we owe the first collected
editions of Aristotle and Plato—but they raised the level of artistic
achievement to new heights, combining grace of typographic form with
fine layout and sometimes with exquisite illustrations. The early Italian
printers also demonstrated the beauty and clarity of the roman letter (as
opposed to the gothic) and introduced the italic letter to printing. It was
they also who popularized the smaller formats, in particular the octavo
size, so that books could be easily carried and consulted by individual
readers. With the exception of devotional works, most books up to this
time—both manuscript and printed—had been made in folio size and
were suitable only for consultation in a library. The use of smaller formats
made the concept of 'polite learning' possible. Thus at the beginning of the
early sixteenth century the *art* of printing (not its technique, which was
well established) had become a branch of communication quite distinct
from manuscript copying.

The age of Aldus and of his printing office in Venice, an age which
brought forth such notable type-cutters and designers as Francesco Griffo
and Geofroy Tory, and which saw the design of letters on a page elevated
to an art form, was succeeded by times when printers forgot the artistic
uses which could be made of their trade. To be sure, the late sixteenth and

Francesco Colonna, *Hypnerotomachia Poliphili*, Venice, Aldus, 1499.

Aldus's type is an elegant roman and the illustrations by an anonymous artist are a sophisticated exercise in perspective and the spare use of lines. Book design had come a long way from early German printing.

OPPOSITE
Apocalypsis Sancti Johannis (the Apocalypse of St. John), a block book printed in Germany, probably before 1470.

Each page is printed from a single block of wood, then coloured by hand. Gutenberg's movable types were quickly seen as providing a more economic method of production. Block books are rare and expensive on the market: this one fetched £198,000 ($345,700) in 1977.

the seventeenth centuries are graced by the printing of many beautiful books, but the slow general decline in standards was not halted by the work of the French family of Estienne (printing in Paris, Geneva and elsewhere) and others who were conscious of the possibilities that the medium offered them. The early eighteenth century, for all its formal elegance, saw printing reach a nadir: printer followed printer in uninspired typography and design, unable or unwilling to break out of the mould in which the printing art had cast itself.

It was, oddly enough, two British printers who revived the notion of printing as an art form. Apart from a few widely separated instances, printers in the British Isles had entirely failed to make a mark on printing history before the establishment of the printing office of Robert and Andrew Foulis in Glasgow in the 1740s. The design of Foulis press books was along traditional lines, with typefaces inspired by previous work (though cut with much more skill). Nevertheless, the Foulis brothers were the first printers for more than a century to swim boldly against the tide of mediocrity which appeared to engulf the art of printing. They printed large numbers of books, and although their best and finest books—for instance their edition of Homer (1756–8)—are expensive, many minor and very attractive works are cheap and easily obtained.

Contemporary with the Foulis brothers, and of much greater influence in the long term, was John Baskerville of Birmingham (1706–75). Baskerville's first book, his magnificent edition of Virgil, was published in 1757, when (in the words of Macaulay) it 'went forth to astonish the librarians of Europe'. With his clean, sharp typefaces and brilliant white paper Baskerville revolutionized the production of fine books, and his example was followed by Giambattista Bodoni (1740–1813) in Parma, and by the Didot press in Paris. He published comparatively few books, although his splendid Bible, printed for the University Press at Cambridge, is relatively common and is within the range of many collectors. Indeed, most of Baskerville's books were printed in large numbers, and ordinary copies (those bound in calf or a lesser material) can be found for less than £500; fine copies bound in morocco and richly decorated are more expensive. Baskerville's genius for typographical design, however, means that his books hold a central place in any library of fine printing; the effects of his revolution remain with us today and are present in every well-designed book.

With the introduction of iron presses in the early nineteenth century, and of powered presses somewhat later, good printing design suffered defeat at the hands of an expanding market. It seems to be as true of the nineteenth century as it had been of the sixteenth, that a rapid growth in production effected a general lowering of standards. One London printer who maintained high standards was Charles Whittingham the younger, who set up shop on his own in 1829 and took over the Chiswick Press from his uncle in 1840. Among his principal customers was William Pickering, and between them they were responsible for perhaps the finest commercial printing of the English nineteenth century.

The word 'commercial' is used advisedly: the Victorian thirst for commerce and profit was to bring its own reaction, in printing as well as in

Q.

HORATII

F L A C C I

O P E R A

PARMAE
IN AEDIBVS PALATINIS
CIƆ IƆ CC LXXXXI
TYPIS BODONIANIS.

Horace, *Opera* [Works], Parma, Bodoni, 1791.

Giambattista Bodoni (1740–1813) was made manager of the Stamperia Reale at Parma in 1768, where he became one of the most influential book and type designers of his age.

Chaucer, *Works*, printed by William Morris at the Kelmscott Press, 1896.

The illustrations were designed by Edward Burne-Jones, and the borders and initials by William Morris. This is the masterpiece of the Kelmscott Press: recent prices have ranged from £3,850 ($6,900) for an 'ordinary' copy to up to £21,450 ($33,900) for a copy in an elaborate jewelled binding.

painting and writing. Although the concept of a 'private press'—a printing shop at the command of a single owner, not obliged to make a profit and run principally as a hobby or to advance his ideals—may be said to have begun with Horace Walpole's press at Strawberry Hill in 1757, it was more than a century before the private press found its classic form in William Morris's Kelmscott Press. The first Kelmscott book, *The Story of the Glittering Plain*, by Morris himself, was issued in 1891, and for artistic achievement and care of execution it represented something new in book work. Part of the inspiration for Morris's ideals came from the Pre-Raphaelite movement, with which he had earlier been associated: but the principal force behind the press was a reaction to the increased mechanization and lifeless design he saw around him. In establishing the tradition of handicraft work against the current of his age, Morris was greatly helped by a group of talented artists and followers, such as Edward Burne-Jones, the typecutter Edward Prince and Sydney Cockerell.

The success of the Kelmscott Press had one unfortunate effect: it split the craft of printing down the middle, and burdened us with a division between 'art' printing (select, beautiful, expensive) and journeyman work

THE DOVES PRESS
№ I THE TERRACE HAMMERSMITH
MDCCCCIII

The Doves Press at Hammersmith, founded by T. J. Cobden-Sanderson in 1900, was one of the greatest of modern private presses, noted for its simple elegance, clarity and good presswork.

(popular, ugly, cheap). Many private presses have been established in the century which followed Morris's new departure, amongst which the most familiar are the Ashendene Press (begun by C. H. St. John Hornby in 1894), the Doves Press (T. J. Cobden-Sanderson, 1900), the Grabhorn Press (Edwin and Robert Grabhorn, 1919) in San Francisco, and the Golden Cockerel Press (Harold Midgely Taylor, 1920). The last two presses were prolific in their output, though always high in standard, and many minor productions are sold for as little as £20–30. Private presses have flourished best in Britain and America, whereas the continental (and especially French) tradition has favoured *livres d'artiste*, which concentrate on the quality of illustrations and luxury of production more than on practical elegance and clarity of typography.

The cockerel device of the Golden Cockerel Press, founded in 1920 by Harold Midgely Taylor.

But the unfortunate side of the private press revolution has been the decline in good book design by commercial publishers. This is most clearly seen in America, where the best printing design today can claim to be the best in the world—and where the worst is the worst, bar none. Modern collectors can amuse themselves with seeking out the finer commercial work of modern times, almost always undervalued when placed against consciously artistic work and frequently available for a few pounds or dollars. Handsomely produced series such as the King Penguins issued in Britain by Allen Lane, already have their enthusiasts, but many more well-made books by undeservedly obscure designers are waiting for the appreciative collector. No book collector interested in design should pass by a bookstall, however unpromising it may seem, for the traces of our culture are to be read in the design of even the most commercial paperback. Good printing has never been the monopoly of lonely artists; it is good business sense, and the results can be appreciated by the layman as easily as by the art student.

ENGLISH LITERATURE

Most people in the English-speaking world have an acquaintance with the history of their own literature, and often a great affection for their favourite authors or periods. Sometimes the seed is sown—on apparently stony ground—at school, where children may gather the idea that Shakespeare and Dickens are dull because they have been taught in an uninteresting manner. But texts studied in youth have a way of returning to haunt the reader in later years. Rudyard Kipling said that his experience at school of the Latin poet Horace made him 'loathe Horace for two years, forget him for twenty, then love him for the rest of my days'.

Kipling is not alone in having returned with love to classical authors he

SHAKESPEARES

COMEDIES,
HISTORIES, &
·TRAGEDIES.

Published according to the True Originall Copies

LONDON
Printed by Isaac Iaggard, and Ed. Blount. 1623.

William Shakespeare, *Comedies,
Histories, & Tragedies*, London, 1623.

The 'First Folio' edition of Shakespeare's
plays is the most important and
expensive of English books. Most copies
are now in institutional libraries, and
copies at auction are very uncommon:
this copy made £88,000 ($206,000) in
1980.

once hated; but now that so little Latin or Greek is taught to children the
very foundations for collecting such literature have crumbled. When an
eighteenth- or nineteenth-century gentleman formed his library, he
would naturally want a representative selection of the best classical
authors; today his equivalent may want to represent literature mainly
through his native language, for that was the literature which was most
deeply ingrained in his youth.

A conspectus of English literature based on printed books contemporary with the authors would have to omit one of its greatest names,
Geoffrey Chaucer (1345–1400). The earliest editions of Chaucer—those
printed by Caxton about 1476 and about 1484—date from over three-
quarters of a century after the poet's death, and are in any case beyond the
reach of collectors today since almost all copies are now held by public
libraries. Editions of the sixteenth century (of which there are several,
beginning with William Thynne's edition of 1532), whilst being an
unsatisfactory substitute for a Caxton or a contemporary edition, provide
the best the modern collector can find. Chaucer's obscure contemporary,
William Langland, was not printed at all until 1550; and even then the
editions of his great poem *Piers Plowman* are less than accurate, and
although comparatively early can only be a poor substitute for a
contemporary manuscript copy. Collectors of more modest means will
have to be satisfied with shabby or imperfect copies even of these
editions, although perfect examples in good condition can be found by the
more persistent.

It seems invidious to pass hurriedly over the major part of the English
sixteenth century, but whilst figures such as John Skelton, Sir Thomas
Wyatt, Sir Thomas Elyot and others are admired by more than specialists,
it is the full flowering of English literature under Elizabeth I in the latter
part of the century that catches the imagination of most collectors. The
great enthusiasm for the Shakespearian period displayed by American
collectors early this century—notably Henry Clay Folger and Henry E.
Huntington, both founders of great research libraries—has made collecting in this area very expensive and usually unrewarding. Nevertheless,
too many collectors have shied away from it under the impression that
nothing remains that is affordable: many classic books of the period are
still quite obtainable with a little patience, and whilst the best copies will
always fetch substantially higher prices, first editions even of works such
as Edmund Spenser's *Faerie Queene* (in two volumes, 1590 and 1596) and
Sir Philip Sidney's *Arcadia* (1590) can be acquired by those wishing to
stretch their purses on occasion.

Shakespeare's works in the earliest editions have always commanded
the highest prices, with pride of place going to the 'First Folio', the folio
edition of his plays published in 1623, seven years after his death. About
half of the plays appeared for the first time in this edition, and for these the
First Folio remains the most authoritative text. By the standards of the
period this is a common book—folio-sized books nearly always survive
best—but the great demand has meant that most copies are in public
libraries; those which remain on the open market fetch astronomic prices,
particularly if they are in good condition. The First Folio was preceded by

a number of quarto editions—short books, simply printed. These are now very rare, and there is little point in trying to collect them unless you have immense resources of both time and money. But, as we have already mentioned, collectors of more modest ambitions can sometimes find Restoration and eighteenth-century editions of Shakespeare for sale. The liberalization of the English stage in 1660 encouraged the rediscovery of Shakespeare, with many adaptations being made by John Dryden and other significant writers of the time. A number of editions were printed, and plays were published separately for the first time. The story of Shakespeare's texts can be pursued into the eighteenth century, with the first 'edited' edition by Nicholas Rowe (1709), the rival editions of Alexander Pope (1723–5) and Lewis Theobald (1733), and, later, that of Samuel Johnson (1765).

Dramatic texts of the late sixteenth century—those of Shakespeare's contemporaries such as Christopher Marlowe and Thomas Kyd—are extremely rare, but those of the next century are not, and copies of many plays printed in the reign of Charles I (1625–49)—but before the outbreak of the English Civil War in 1641, when the theatres were closed—are surprisingly easily obtainable, and are still part of the Elizabethan tradition. Collected editions of an author (Shakespeare excepted, as ever) can often be bought for comparatively modest sums. Ben Jonson (1572–1637) was one of the first to favour this form of edition, publishing his own *Works* in 1616. (This was republished with a second volume, in 1639–40, at the time of his death.) The plays of Francis Beaumont and John Fletcher were also published in a collected edition, in 1647, another impressive folio which looks more expensive than it often is.

The theatre should not, however, be allowed to dominate our perception of the English Renaissance in book form: a vigorous cultural undercurrent produced a mass of literature, both noble and ephemeral, both poetry and prose. Many ephemeral pieces have vanished for ever or have survived by chance in larger collections. The greater works, the solemn or the pretentious—always more highly regarded by their authors and contemporaries than the fly-by-night literature of the streets—will nowadays often fetch the lower prices.

The character of the English press changed abruptly with the outbreak of Civil War. Nearly all the presses were in London, and had until then been tightly controlled. As London was a city firmly in the grip of the anti-monarchist parliament, royal censorship vanished and a flood of publications sprang forth to meet the urgent demand for news and to satisfy the appetite for controversy. English printing was suddenly liberalized and never returned to its stuffy past. At the centre of this ferment of ideas and opinions was John Milton (1608–74), the Latin secretary (which meant that he dealt with correspondence in Latin, mostly to foreign governments) to the Commonwealth Council of State. Milton's works in prose, mainly controversial and written in the heat of the dispute, date from this period. His poetry was to a large extent written before the outbreak of hostilities—his *Poems* of 1645 and *Comus* of 1637 are rare and highly priced volumes—but his great work, *Paradise Lost*, was not written until after the Restoration when, escaping Royalist retribution, he had settled

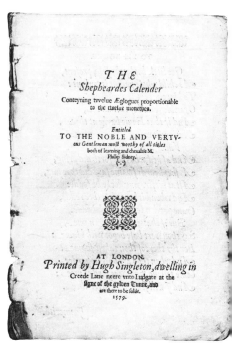

Edmund Spenser, *The Shepheardes Calender*, London, 1579.

This is the first book published by Spenser: only six copies were known until 1980, when this one was bought for a few pounds in a country sale in Derbyshire. Resold at Christie's in London, it made £41,800 ($100,320), a handsome profit for the fortunate owner.

into poetic retirement. The finished poem, the greatest epic in the English language, was published in 1667 and although it sold slowly (it was reissued several times with new title pages substituted) it was quickly recognized as something unique in the English poetry of the time. The second edition of Milton's *Poems*, published in 1673, includes many new poems published for the first time, such as his famous sonnet on his blindness ('When I consider how my light is spent'): like Milton's other late books this is still obtainable by modern collectors for relatively modest sums, whilst the early works are extremely rare.

Other poets of the Restoration find less favour with modern readers. Dryden, Shadwell, Sedley, Tate, Roscommon—with the exception of John Dryden (1631–1700) these are names largely unfamiliar to modern collectors, and in consequence their plays and poems are undervalued in today's market. Yet they were the inheritors of the Elizabethan tradition, and strove to renew the language on 'correct' lines—an attempt continued in the eighteenth century by Pope and Johnson. As inevitably happens with a collecting area which has ceased to be fashionable, prices have stabilized or dropped, and most books of the Restoration, relatively common when set alongside the literature before 1640, are priced low enough for many collectors to be able to aspire to a representative collection.

The figures of Alexander Pope (1688–1744) and Samuel Johnson (1709–84) dominate the English eighteenth century, for the collector as for the literary historian: Pope, the controversial poet, effortlessly fending off the attacks of his opponents; Johnson, the man of all genres, able to write a Dictionary (two large folio volumes, 1755), poetry (*London: A Poem*, 1738, and *The Vanity of Human Wishes*, 1749), a journalist and biographer as well as editor and critic. Whilst the highlights of literary

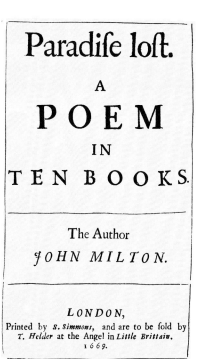

John Milton, *Paradise Lost*, London, 1667 and 1669.

Milton's epic poem sold slowly on first publication in 1667, and it was reissued several times with new title pages. Copies with the early title page fetch high prices, whereas the later issues have sold for as little as £660 ($1,500)—the price this 1669 issue (right) sold for in 1980.

[Jonathan Swift], *Travels into Several Remote Nations of the World*, 2 volumes, 1726.

Swift's 'Gulliver's Travels' was published in 1726 as though it were a genuine autobiography. There are many difficult issue points which affect the price, but copies are occasionally found for as little as £600 ($750).

achievement in this period have always·been eagerly bought, collectors in recent years have searched in greater depth and more widely than ever before. In this they are aided and encouraged by the availability of more sophisticated bibliographies, which make collecting more rewarding by telling the collector what is already known and how common a certain book may be: perhaps the most notable recent work is the catalogue by David Foxon of all the separately printed English poetry of the first half of the century—a daunting pair of volumes, full of new information on the exact bibliography of thousands of books, based on the author's personal examination of many copies.

As so often happens when the reference works for a period are improved, the prices for many eighteenth-century books have shot up in recent years, with attention not being confined to the traditionally collected authors. Famous works like Daniel Defoe's *Robinson Crusoe* (1719) continue to attract high prices, especially good copies, but the variety and complex bibliography of other works by Defoe (most of his writing was published anonymously) has tended to put off the collector, who has little hope of making a complete library of his author's works. Jonathan Swift, by contrast, is well served with a good and complete bibliography, and this has helped to maintain a steady rise in the price of his works.

The later eighteenth century is usually thought of as the province of Samuel Johnson, but his reputation and genius should not be allowed to obscure contemporaries who have been quite as much admired in our day as in their own: Horace Walpole (1717–97), the great letter-writer, advocate of Gothic revival architecture, owner of the Strawberry Hill private press, and author of the first 'Gothic horror' novel, *The Castle of*

[William Wordsworth and Samuel Taylor Coleridge,] *Lyrical Ballads*, Bristol, 1798, and London, 1798.

Like *Paradise Lost*, Wordsworth and Coleridge's epoch-making *Lyrical Ballads* was originally published, anonymously, with different title pages. The Bristol issue, the first, is known from only a few copies and none has come on the market for many years. The London issue is comparatively common, and the second edition (1800, with its important preface) still more so.

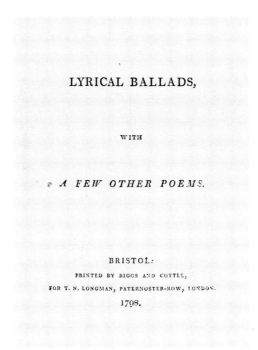

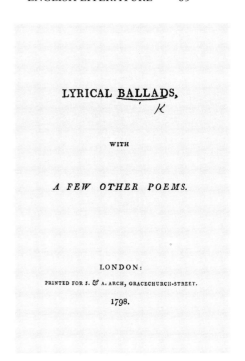

Otranto (1764); Oliver Goldsmith (1728–74), author of *The Vicar of Wakefield* (1765) and *She Stoops to Conquer* (1773); and, of course, Edward Gibbon (1737–94), whose monumental *History of the Decline and Fall of the Roman Empire* first appeared in six volumes between 1776 and 1788.

The romantic rebellion in literature at the end of the eighteenth century is crystallized in William Wordsworth's and Samuel Taylor Coleridge's *Lyrical Ballads* (1798). But this is an instance of a second edition also being important to the collector, for it was not until 1800, when a second volume was added and the first volume revised, that the famous preface, which has been called the manifesto of the romantic movement, was added by the authors. With this book, as with a number of other seminal books, it is legitimate to feel that the revised edition is preferable to the first edition, although both have their importance.

For collectors of English literature the nineteenth century is sharply divided into the novelists and the poets. The printing and publication of the novelists has been closely studied, and even the minor figures have been avidly collected: this is partly because of the influence of the English collector Michael Sadleir, whose passion for nineteenth-century fiction resulted in an unparalleled collection of novels in their original bindings (now at the University of California at Los Angeles). Collectors beginning their career with the nineteenth century might be well advised to start with the better-known names such as Dickens, Thackeray or Wilkie Collins before exploring the less well-known authors. Most of Dickens's novels were first published 'in parts'—that is, in twenty or so monthly numbers which the purchaser might then have bound up into volumes. 'First edition in book form' denotes a novel's first appearance as published in a single book. Curiously, good copies in parts are easier to find than really fine copies of these secondary editions, and since the latter are almost always cheaper one can assemble an interestingly difficult collection by keeping only to the cloth-bound 'book-form' editions.

Minor fiction of the period is a very different field. Most popular novels of the mid-century were published in three volumes, and are known as 'three-decker' novels. They represented the staple business of the circulating libraries, and many of the most collected novelists are minor figures indeed—how many students of English literature have heard of Rhoda Broughton or F. Marion Crawford? Collectors today concentrate on such novelists partly for their modern obscurity compared with their past popularity, but also for the attractive and adventurous design of the bindings, so redolent of the age.

Modern collections of the nineteenth-century poets are, by contrast, largely confined to the great names, some of whose first editions are now very difficult to find in fine condition, or at all. The major poets of the mid-nineteenth century are satisfyingly cheap for the new collector—fine copies of most later Tennyson first editions can be found for under twenty pounds—but the more experienced collector will seek a harder quarry, for example an association copy or a special printing. Minor poets, in contrast with the novelists, are not much collected and, because there are few works of reference, present considerable bibliographical problems: who is to say whether this is the true first edition, or if that is really the original binding?

A note of caution: the bibliography of nineteenth-century English poetry has also suffered from the attentions of T. J. Wise, the bibliographer eminent in his own day but since revealed as a forger of evidence (see pp. 45–6). Wise's bibliographies of such figures as Swinburne, Byron and many others are still indispensable, but they must be used carefully, since not only do they list his forgeries as genuine, but the collector's pride overcame any instinct for accuracy in the bibliographer: many items in his own collections are distinguished for mention as 'special' issues without good evidence, or are described as rarer than later scholars have found them to be.

It is with their own century, however, that most modern collectors of literature begin their careers, since these are the books with which they feel most instinctive sympathy and the texts which they are most likely to have already on their shelves. Yet collectors of modern first editions should beware of the rapid changes of fashion which can leave their highly prized (and highly priced) purchases either impossible to resell or saleable only at a spectacular loss. This problem besets every collector, but rapid changes of taste affect the market for moderns more than any other market, since the 'track record' is still to be established: some prices paid at auction leave even the specialist dealers gasping with astonishment. More than with most books, the collecting of modern first editions is a matter for your own enthusiasm: if you really think the book is worth so much of your money, then it must be a good 'investment' since you are investing primarily in your own satisfaction. The rules remain the same: stick only to good condition, and buy the best copies you can afford. A few special points ought also to be borne in mind, and the most important

William Makepeace Thackeray, *The Virginians*, London, 1857–9.

Like Dickens, Thackeray published his novels in monthly parts; their paper wrappers are now usually frail and often torn. Editions of Thackeray's works in parts are quite cheap (with the exception of *Vanity Fair*) and go for as little as £150 ($200) at auction.

A collection of novels by Anthony Trollope in their original cloth bindings.

Publishers issued novels in handsome and adventurously designed bindings in the later nineteenth century. The cloth was not very strong and it is now difficult to find them in good condition.

of these concerns the dust-jacket: if the book was issued with one you should always try to buy a copy which retains it, since this is now considered to be an essential part of the book as published. Occasionally a collector or dealer will tell you that he dislikes the fad for keeping dust-jackets, and that a book is worth the same without one. The consensus of opinion in today's market is, however, against this view, and to disregard the sentiment of other collectors may be to throw your money away. Speculative though it may be, and disdained by some though it certainly is, there is a noble aspect to the collecting of modern literature, for one is taking part in the creation of a literary reputation (some would say, the making of a coffin) for one's favourite authors. To enshrine them in a collection is surely a desire natural enough and worthy enough to deserve praise.

Buying one's national literature, of whatever period, is one of the oldest forms of book collecting; it is surely the most widespread. We fasten instinctively onto our linguistic and cultural inheritance, and find our own identities by what we read and collect as much as by the clothes we wear or the language we speak.

SCIENTIFIC AND MEDICAL BOOKS

Old scientific and medical books are documents of social and intellectual history, as well as being part of the histories of their own subjects, and one or both of these ideas forms the basis of most collections. As documents of social change it is usually the 'great' books which are collected, the books which can be seen to mark turning-points in the history of ideas and in our conception of man's place in nature. The most obvious examples are Nicolaus Copernicus's *De revolutionibus orbium coelestium* (Nuremberg, 1543), which marks the acceptance in modern times of the heliocentric planetary system and thus contains the statement—heretical in its day— that the world is not at the centre of the universe; and Charles Darwin's *On*

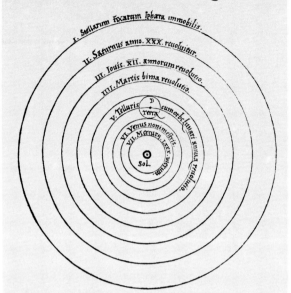

NICOLAI COPERNICI

net, in quo terram cum orbe lunari tanquam epicyclo contineri
diximus. Quinto loco Venus nono menfe reducitur. Sextum
deniq; locum Mercurius tenet, octuaginta dierum fpacio circũ
currens, In medio uero omnium refidet Sol. Quis enim in hoc

pulcherimo templo lampadem hanc in alio uel meliori loco po
neret, quàm unde totum fimul pofsit illuminare? Siquidem non
inepte quidam lucernam mundi, alñ mentem, alñ rectorem uo=
cant. Trimegiftus uifibilem Deum, Sophoclis Electra intuentẽ
omnia. Ita profecto tanquam in folio re gali Sol refidens circum
agentem gubernat Aftrorum familiam. Tellus quoqʒ minime
fraudatur lunari minifterio, fed ut Ariftoteles de animalibus
ait, maximã Luna cũ terra cognationẽ habet. Concipit interea à
Sole terra, & impregnatur annuo partu. Inuenimus igitur fub
hac

Nicolaus Copernicus, *De revolutionibus orbium coelestium*, Nuremberg, 1543. Woodcut of the heliocentric universe.

The book which established the notion of the sun as the centre of the universe. It is thought that 500 copies of Copernicus's book were printed, and even after 440 years there is still at least one copy every year on the market. But because of the book's significance copies command high prices: one in a later binding made £14,850 ($36,234) at auction in 1980, and a copy in a contemporary pigskin binding sold for DM 146,050 (£37,258; $57,377) in 1983.

the *Origin of Species by means of Natural Selection* (1859), which first suggested that the higher species were not directly created by God but evolved slowly from inferior forms of life. Other 'great' books are those which mark scientific advances which have materially affected our daily lives, for example Edward Jenner's *An Inquiry into the Causes and Effects of the Variolae Vaccinae* (1798), which laid the scientific basis for smallpox inoculation, and H. R. Hertz's *Untersuchungen über die Ausbreitung der Elektrischen Kraft* (Leipzig, 1892), which paved the way for radio and television.

Science and medicine are perhaps not held today in the same esteem by the sort of people who collect books as, say, literature or music. This is no doubt the legacy of William Morris and of the Edwardian reaction to Victorian 'progress'. But to the educated, especially the self-educated, reader of the nineteenth century, each new scientific advance was the harbinger of greater comfort and prosperity. The miner's safety-lamp, scientific agriculture, the electric telegraph, mass production of steel and gas, electric lighting, photography, aniline dyes, anaesthetics, antiseptic

Charles Darwin, *On the Origin of Species*, London, 1859, with Florence Nightingale, *Notes on Nursing*, London [December 1859], and one part of Charles Dickens, *A Tale of Two Cities*, published the same year.

Probably no two books of the century had so profound an effect on Victorian culture as Darwin's *Origin of Species* and Nightingale's *Notes on Nursing*—or, with Samuel Smiles's *Self Help*, also printed in 1859, were more widely read. The writer Harriet Martineau remarked early in 1860 that she saw the *Origin* on every young gentleman's table and *Notes on Nursing* on every young lady's.

surgery, sanitation and hospital reform: these were some of the tangible results of scientific endeavour in the later eighteenth and in the nineteenth centuries. The progress in engineering not strictly attributable to scientific discovery was even greater. In pure science this was the age of Priestley, Franklin, Lavoisier, Faraday, Helmholtz, Maxwell, Pasteur and Schwann. And then there was natural history, that gentle pursuit beloved of women and clergymen, in which science could turn its back on progress: paradoxically, it was a naturalist, Charles Darwin, who made the greatest single advance in nineteenth-century science.

The literature of science in the Victorian era and before is particularly rich: collectors can approach it both through the technical treatises written for experts (still surprisingly readable) and through the many educational and popular books, which are of the greatest value as social documents. Today we are wary of assuming that scientific progress is always beneficial, but our forebears had no such doubts about the power of science and medicine to improve the world. New discoveries were reported in journals, and were eagerly discussed, criticized and explained in books written for all sorts of readers—experts, laymen and children.

The Great Scientific Books

Collecting the 'great books' in the history of science and the cult of the first edition are relatively recent phenomena. A key event influencing collectors was the exhibition held in 1934 at the University of California at Berkeley (near San Francisco), which presented the collection of books in the history of science formed by Herbert McLean Evans. The show was entitled 'An Exhibition of First Editions of Epochal Achievements in the History of Science'. We need not dwell on the infelicity of the phrase 'epochal achievements': the point is that the idea of the 'first edition' and of the 'epochal achievement' is still with us and is very relevant to the collecting of antiquarian books in the history of science. Although he wrote with an exaggeration born of enthusiasm, McLean Evans made some important points in the Introduction to his exhibition catalogue:

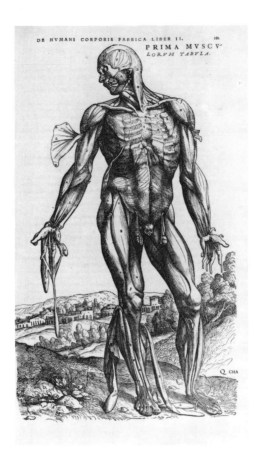

'The collection of first editions, one of the chief cults of bibliomania, is perhaps more justifiable in the realm of scientific "firsts" than in any other territory invaded by the hobby. The precise form of an achievement in *belles-lettres* is of course the very reason for its being, and is preserved in the abundant reprints by means of which man reverentially ministers to his spirit. ... Reprints of scientific works, as originally enunciated, are rare. Yet it is only by consulting the first form of a scientific achievement that one can hope to observe the origin and change of ideas. But, more than this, it may be maintained that one cannot adequately understand any scientific subject without knowledge of the manner in which our present conceptions were established.'

The McLean Evans exhibition has inspired other exhibitions and catalogues, the most sophisticated and influential of which was the exhibition 'Printing and the Mind of Man'. This was based on the collection of Ian Fleming (author of the James Bond books), and formed part of the International Printing Machinery and Allied Trades Exhibition (IPEX) in 1963. The original exhibition catalogue was expanded and published in a book of the same title which has become a standard work of reference, encouraging the cult of the 'epochal book', and having a profound effect on the prices of some of the books it describes. Collectors and booksellers tend to use *Printing and the Mind of Man* and similar catalogues as a guide to the importance of certain books, and the inclusion of a particular work confers on it a seal of approval. But this dependence creates obvious problems: our perspective on history may not be the same as that of the compilers, or they may have overlooked certain books; or an important book which they wished to include may not have been available for exhibition. Tempting though it is to rely on these catalogues, no serious collector can afford to let them choose his books for him: an open mind is always essential.

Every collector will soon have his own list of significant books which should be included among the greats but are not to be found in these catalogues. Nevertheless, such catalogues form a useful point of reference. Besides the McLean Evans catalogue and *Printing and the Mind of Man*, booksellers frequently refer to Bern Dibner's *Heralds of Science* (1955, revised edition 1980) and to Harrison D. Horblit's *One Hundred Books Famous in Science*, published for the Grolier Club in 1964.

The essence of the 'great book' is that it transcends the limits of its particular subject area. Such books may not have universal appeal, but they are of universal importance—and, with the usual moderating effect of comparative scarcity, they are consequently highly valued. Of course, some great discoveries were understood as crucial from the beginning and comparatively large editions were produced; more importantly, these books were treasured by successive owners so that survival rates are high (as in the case of Copernicus, Newton and Darwin, for example). Others were hardly noticed at the time and are now very rare: William Harvey's *De motu cordis*, published in Frankfurt in 1628, the book which established the circulation of the blood as a fact, is often called the greatest book in the history of medicine, but it is a well-known rarity; so is Gregor

William Harvey, *De motu cordis*, Frankfurt, 1628.

This small pamphlet announces Harvey's discovery, apparently obvious but at the time revolutionary, of the circulation of the blood. This is the Honeyman copy, sold at auction in 1979 for £96,800 ($205,430), an auction record for a scientific book.

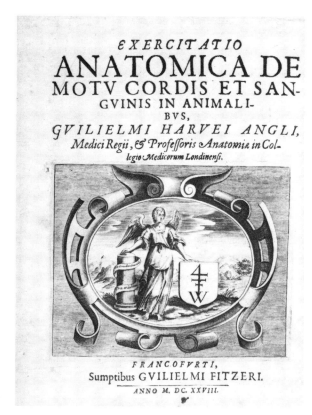

Mendel's paper of 1866 on the principles of heredity—work which remained unnoticed until 1900.

First Editions in Science and Medicine

When is a first edition not a first edition? In scientific and medical book collecting there are two kinds of first edition which are not quite what they seem. First, some important scientific discoveries were announced before the author's definitive account, so that the 'first edition' is not the crucial document that one would like it to be. Copernicus's *De revolutionibus* of 1543 was not the first demonstration to the scientific community of his planetary theory, for it had been described by his pupil Georg Rheticus in a small pamphlet entitled *De libris revolutionum Copernici . . . narratio prima* ('A First Account of the Books of Copernicus about Revolutions') published three years before. Like several other first announcements this is a very rare book indeed and in 1980, when the last copy was auctioned, it fetched more than five times as much as the copy of *De revolutionibus* sold in the same year (£80,300, compared with £14,850).

The second difficulty with scientific and medical 'first editions' is that the first announcement may well be in a journal. Towards the end of the nineteenth century it became (and has remained) almost invariable practice to publish first in the journals and reserve a fuller analysis for a book, or a review of a number of journal articles. With more recent discoveries it is therefore wise always to ask 'Was this research previously published in another form?' If the book is a reprint of one or more journal articles it should be called the 'first book edition' or some such phrase, but the facts are not always easy to ascertain.

Where a discovery is published in a journal the collector may be able to obtain a short run of the journal bound into its annual volumes or the single volume containing the paper in question. This has the attraction of showing the work in its original context; on the other hand runs of journals are bulky and odd volumes somehow unsatisfying. To overcome this, booksellers and collectors have resorted to the practice of pulling out the few pages that make up the desired article and binding them as a slim volume, or just keeping them in a folder; but to bibliographic purists this is a barbaric practice. The best forms in which to collect a journal article are, unfortunately, both rare: these are the individual unbound journal 'part' (like a single number of a magazine) in which the paper originally appeared, or an offprint (confusingly called a 'reprint' in North America) originally given to the author for private distribution.

Scientific publishing in journal form began in the 1660s with the *Philosophical Transactions* of the Royal Society of London, the *Acta eruditorum* in Germany and the *Journal des sçavans* in Paris; by the middle of the eighteenth century it had become common practice for the publishers to provide authors with a small number of copies of their article printed separately as a pamphlet to circulate among their friends. Usually these were printed from the same type as the journal and were circulated before the journal, making them the true 'first editions', even though the type had sometimes been reset for the offprint. The number of

Alessandro Piccolomini, *De la sfera del mondo*, and *De le stelle fisse*, Venice, 1540. Woodcut.

The 48 star maps in this book are the first ever printed. This attractive book seems to be somewhat undervalued, selling for around £500 ($625) at auction.

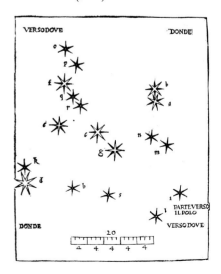

Bernard Siegfried Albinus, *Tabulae sceleti et musculorum corporis humani*, London, 1747. Engraving.

This large folio anatomical atlas was first published in Leyden in the same year as the London edition, with plates engraved by Wandelaar. Although the quality of the engraving in the English edition is not as good, the plates are still splendid and the book sells for £600–700 ($750–875) at auction, about a third of what the much rarer Dutch edition would make.

offprints given to an author was generally limited, and as they were often signed by the author for presentation to close colleagues they have a special immediacy and importance as the means of communication among a small group of workers in a specialist field. A note of caution: not all offprints are rare. Einstein's later papers were evidently in great demand and the publishers of the *Annalen der Physik* and other journals made large editions of the offprints. *Die Grundlage der allgemeinen Relativitätstheorie* (1916), the General Theory of Relativity itself, in its separate form, is not really an offprint at all as it was published for general sale, not just for private circulation. This does not of course make these papers any less interesting but it does mean that they command lower prices than might otherwise be expected: the separate edition of *Die Grundlage*, for example, sells for only a few hundred pounds, far less than we would expect for a work of such fundamental importance.

Collecting by Subject

The inspiration for all collectors of scientific books should be Sir Isaac Newton's modest asseveration: 'If I have seen further than others it is because I have stood on the shoulders of giants.' It is the cumulative nature of scientific discovery that makes scientific and medical book collecting so fascinating. Few books stand on their own, independent of their contemporaries and predecessors: they almost invariably have roots which can be traced in earlier books and their new ideas can be seen to bear fruit in later works. Newton himself had a fine working library (much of it now preserved in Trinity College Library, Cambridge) and he knew his giants through their books. Modern book collecting is only different because of the emphasis on 'first editions', and this can easily be carried too far in collecting a single subject—say astronomy, or ophthalmology, or surgical anatomy—in the history of science. As we have seen, collecting 'great books' implies collecting 'first editions', but it is wrong to be rigidly insistent on first editions in forming a subject collection. Of course the first edition has a special historical as well as a romantic importance, but a subject collection (encompassing the more common as well as the rarer books) represents the internal history of that subject, and it is contained as much, if not more, in later editions, for an author's definitive text is usually more important to the subsequent history of the subject than his first attempt. Newton's library was not a library of first editions, and the collector often gets a better picture of scientific progress if a collection is not artificially limited to first appearances.

Anyone with a special knowledge of or interest in a particular scientific discipline is likely to want to collect the books associated with the history of that subject. In some areas there are good histories and bibliographies which can help in identifying the most important available books. Chemistry, for example, is well served with the massive *History of Chemistry* by J. R. Partington and the catalogues of the collections of Henry Carrington Bolton, Denis I. Duveen and John Ferguson. Several histories of mathematics and astronomy have been written, but the bibliographies are satisfactory in only a few specialist areas or periods and there is a lot to collect: a surprisingly large number of interesting and very beautifully printed sixteenth-century books can be found for one, two or three hundred pounds, whilst the less well-known eighteenth-century and later books may be obtainable for a fraction of those amounts. Newton and the works directly influenced by him are central to any collection in the history of physics, and the books are well documented. But in any of these fields each collection will have its own emphasis and it is almost impossible to form a collection without discovering new facts and previously unnoticed relationships in the internal history of the chosen subject. This is even more true in relatively unexplored subjects and periods, for example nineteenth-century mathematics and logic, and many areas of technology and engineering. Popular science, too, has not been properly researched and the books are quite inexpensive.

In medicine, book collecting is better developed than in the other physical sciences, for medical books of the past have a special place in modern practice in addition to their purely historical value. The first accurate description of a particular disease, or a physiological structure, becomes the 'classic' description to which all others must refer, and such diseases are often named after the authors of these classic works. Thus Hodgkin's disease and Bell's palsy, the fallopian tubes and graafian follicles are named after Thomas Hodgkin, Charles Bell, Gabriele Fallopius and Regner de Graaf, in whose books and papers they were first accurately described. Furthermore, good descriptions of cases are never out of date and may be useful today in comparing one case with another.

The bible of modern medical book collecting is 'Garrison and Morton' (Leslie T. Morton, *A Medical Bibliography*, fourth edition, 1983). First published in 1943, this work sets out to list, and to a remarkable degree succeeds in doing so, the most important works in the history of medicine in a classified list of nearly 8,000 entries, often with useful annotations. The entries in Garrison and Morton in any subject area provide a useful foundation on which the specialist collector can build.

AMERICANA AND AUSTRALIANA

Collecting national literature, whether it be French or Swedish, South African or Spanish, has a logical extension in collecting books about the country, or books which have been significant in its development. Such works are often referred to by adding the suffix 'ana' to the country's name—Braziliana, for example, or South Americana. These names, though cumbersome, describe a special genre of collecting which is widespread among collectors, especially those from countries of the New World. To a collector of Americana the seventeenth-century poet Anne Bradstreet (1612–72) is interesting more as one of the earliest poets writing and living on the continent of America than for her actual poetic talent. The Australian who collects books on his native country will be more attracted by John Gould's *Birds of Australia* (1840–8) than, say, the same author's *Humming-Birds* (1849–61), even though the latter may be generally

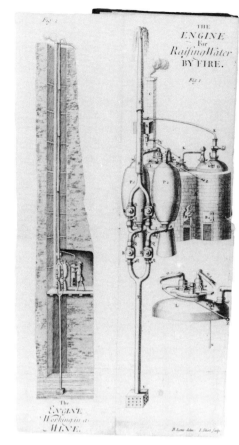

Thomas Savery, *The Miners Friend*, London, 1702.

The description of the first steam pump, the first useful application of the force of steam for mechanical purposes. A copy has recently been offered by a dealer for $3,500 (£2,800).

OPPOSITE

A Declaration by the Representatives of the United States of America, in General Congress Assembled. Philadelphia, John Dunlap, [1776].

The first printing of the fundamental document of the history of the United States. Only 22 copies are now known of this simple broadside, and but two remain in private ownership.

In CONGRESS, July 4, 1776.

A DECLARATION

By the REPRESENTATIVES of the

UNITED STATES OF AMERICA,

In GENERAL CONGRESS ASSEMBLED.

WHEN in the Course of human Events, it becomes neceffary for one People to diffolve the Political Bands which have connected them with another, and to affume among the Powers of the Earth, the feparate and equal Station to which the Laws of Nature and of Nature's God entitle them, a decent Refpect to the Opinions of Mankind requires that they fhould declare the caufes which impel them to the Separation.

We hold thefe Truths to be felf-evident, that all Men are created equal, that they are endowed by their Creator with certain unalienable Rights, that among thefe are Life, Liberty, and the Purfuit of Happinefs--That to fecure thefe Rights, Governments are inftituted among Men, deriving their juft Powers from the Confent of the Governed, that whenever any Form of Government becomes deftructive of thefe Ends, it is the Right of the People to alter or to abolifh it, and to inftitute new Government, laying its Foundation on fuch Principles, and organizing its Powers in fuch Form, as to them fhall feem moft likely to effect their Safety and Happinefs. Prudence, indeed, will dictate that Governments long eftablifhed fhould not be changed for light and tranfient Caufes; and accordingly all Experience hath fhewn, that Mankind are more difpofed to fuffer, while Evils are fufferable, than to right themfelves by abolifhing the Forms to which they are accuftomed. But when a long Train of Abufes and Ufurpations, purfuing invariably the fame Object, evinces a Defign to reduce them under abfolute Defpotifm, it is their Right, it is their Duty, to throw off fuch Government, and to provide new Guards for their future Security. Such has been the patient Sufferance of thefe Colonies; and fuch is now the Neceffity which conftrains them to alter their former Syftems of Government. The Hiftory of the prefent King of Great-Britain is a Hiftory of repeated Injuries and Ufurpations, all having in direct Object the Eftablifhment of an abfolute Tyranny over thefe States. To prove this, let Facts be fubmitted to a candid World.

He has refufed his Affent to Laws, the moft wholefome and neceffary for the public Good.

He has forbidden his Governors to pafs Laws of immediate and preffing Importance, unlefs fufpended in their Operation till his Affent fhould be obtained; and when fo fufpended, he has utterly neglected to attend to them.

He has refufed to pafs other Laws for the Accommodation of large Diftricts of People, unlefs thofe People would relinquifh the Right of Reprefentation in the Legiflature, a Right ineftimable to them, and formidable to Tyrants only.

He has called together Legiflative Bodies at Places unufual, uncomfortable, and diftant from the Depofitory of their public Records, for the fole Purpofe of fatiguing them into Compliance with his Meafures.

He has diffolved Reprefentative Houfes repeatedly, for oppofing with manly Firmnefs his Invafions on the Rights of the People.

He has refufed for a long Time, after fuch Diffolutions, to caufe others to be elected; whereby the Legiflative Powers, incapable of Annihilation, have returned to the People at large for their exercife; the State remaining in the mean time expofed to all the Dangers of Invafion from without, and Convulfions within.

He has endeavoured to prevent the Population of thefe States; for that Purpofe obftructing the Laws for Naturalization of Foreigners; refufing to pafs others to encourage their Migrations hither, and raifing the Conditions of new Appropriations of Lands.

He has obftructed the Adminiftration of Juftice, by refufing his Affent to Laws for eftablifhing Judiciary Powers.

He has made Judges dependent on his Will alone, for the Tenure of their Offices, and the Amount and Payment of their Salaries.

He has erected a Multitude of new Offices, and fent hither Swarms of Officers to harrafs our People, and eat out their Subftance.

He has kept among us, in Times of Peace, Standing Armies, without the confent of our Legiflatures.

He has affected to render the Military independent of and fuperior to the Civil Power.

He has combined with others to fubject us to a Jurifdiction foreign to our Conftitution, and unacknowledged by our Laws; giving his Affent to their Acts of pretended Legiflation:

For quartering large Bodies of Armed Troops among us:

For protecting them, by a mock Trial, from Punifhment for any Murders which they fhould commit on the Inhabitants of thefe States:

For cutting off our Trade with all Parts of the World:

For impofing Taxes on us without our Confent:

For depriving us, in many Cafes, of the Benefits of Trial by Jury:

For tranfporting us beyond Seas to be tried for pretended Offences:

For abolifhing the free Syftem of Englifh Laws in a neighbouring Province, eftablifhing therein an arbitrary Government, and enlarging its Boundaries, fo as to render it at once an Example and fit Inftrument for introducing the fame abfolute Rule into thefe Colonies:

For taking away our Charters, abolifhing our moft valuable Laws, and altering fundamentally the Forms of our Governments:

For fufpending our own Legiflatures, and declaring themfelves invefted with Power to legiflate for us in all Cafes whatfoever.

He has abdicated Government here, by declaring us out of his Protection and waging War againft us.

He has plundered our Seas, ravaged our Coafts, burnt our Towns, and deftroyed the Lives of our People.

He is, at this Time, tranfporting large Armies of foreign Mercenaries to compleat the Works of Death, Defolation, and Tyranny, already begun with circumftances of Cruelty and Perfidy, fcarcely paralleled in the moft barbarous Ages, and totally unworthy the Head of a civilized Nation.

He has conftrained our fellow Citizens taken Captive on the high Seas to bear Arms againft their Country, to become the Executioners of their Friends and Brethren, or to fall themfelves by their Hands.

He has excited domeftic Infurrections amongft us, and has endeavoured to bring on the Inhabitants of our Frontiers, the mercilefs Indian Savages, whofe known Rule of Warfare, is an undiftinguifhed Deftruction, of all Ages, Sexes and Conditions.

In every ftage of thefe Oppreffions we have Petitioned for Redrefs in the moft humble Terms: Our repeated Petitions have been anfwered only by repeated Injury. A Prince, whofe Character is thus marked by every act which may define a Tyrant, is unfit to be the Ruler of a free People.

Nor have we been wanting in Attentions to our Britifh Brethren. We have warned them from Time to Time of Attempts by their Legiflature to extend an unwarrantable Jurifdiction over us. We have reminded them of the Circumftances of our Emigration and Settlement here. We have appealed to their native Juftice and Magnanimity, and we have conjured them by the Ties of our common Kindred to difavow thefe Ufurpations, which, would inevitably interrupt our Connections and Correfpondence. They too have been deaf to the Voice of Juftice and of Confanguinity. We muft, therefore, acquiefce in the Neceffity, which denounces our Separation, and hold them, as we hold the reft of Mankind, Enemies in War, in Peace, Friends.

We, therefore, the Reprefentatives of the UNITED STATES OF AMERICA, in GENERAL CONGRESS, Affembled, appealing to the Supreme Judge of the World for the Rectitude of our Intentions, do, in the Name, and by Authority of the good People of thefe Colonies, folemnly Publifh and Declare, That thefe United Colonies are, and of Right ought to be, FREE AND INDEPENDENT STATES; that they are abfolved from all Allegiance to the Britifh Crown, and that all political Connection between them and the State of Great-Britain, is and ought to be totally diffolved; and that as FREE AND INDEPENDENT STATES, they have full Power to levy War, conclude Peace, contract Alliances, eftablifh Commerce, and to do all other Acts and Things which INDEPENDENT STATES may of right do. And for the fupport of this Declaration, with a firm Reliance on the Protection of divine Providence, we mutually pledge to each other our Lives, our Fortunes, and our facred Honor.

Signed by ORDER *and in* BEHALF *of the* CONGRESS,

JOHN HANCOCK, PRESIDENT.

ATTEST.
CHARLES THOMSON, SECRETARY.

PHILADELPHIA: PRINTED BY JOHN DUNLAP.

Joseph Lycett, *Views in Australia*, London, 1824.

Lycett's picturesque book is a favourite with connoisseurs of Australiana. Kangaroos sport alongside ostriches in an idyllic antipodean scene.

OPPOSITE
John James Audubon, *The Birds of America*, 5 volumes, London, 1827–38.

A complete set of the magnificent coloured aquatint plates of American birds by Audubon, bound in enormous ('double elephant folio') volumes, was sold in London in 1984 for £1,100,000 ($1,540,000). But two other copies have been sold in recent years, plate by plate, for prices ranging upwards from $1,000 (£800).

thought the finer book. Such an approach may indicate a myopic disregard for books which are quite as worthy as those the collector is seeking; but all book collectors must discriminate according to their passions, and we are all found wanting when judged by others' lights.

When printing with movable types was invented, the world known to Europeans was small and definable. Their knowledge was soon to expand rapidly, with the New World opening before them and the medium of print spreading acquaintance with strange places. Less than forty years after Gutenberg finished his first book, Columbus returned from America with his news of unexplored countries, and the modern world began to take its shape.

Columbus's voyage in 1492 is perhaps the most famous example of a country's 'discovery' by outside settlers and colonizers, but there are of course many others—Australia, South America, and the various countries of Africa. And though we discuss here only the two most popular 'literatures of nationhood', the collector can follow the awakening of many other countries through the medium of print. Books and manuscripts are the most eloquent and appropriate artefacts for illustrating this phase in mankind's history—as they would not be for, say, the recent history of man's exploration of space—because printing was the most effective and immediate form of communication. The collector can gain a real excitement from knowing that his books were indeed agents in altering the map of the world.

Matter from the first presses of any country is likely to be scarce, and the printed matter from the first centuries of European settlement of central and northern America is particularly sought-after. The earliest printed books in Europe are known, as we have seen, as *incunabula*, and the term has been unofficially adopted by some countries and even by areas within countries to denote books produced during the period when the national printing press was in its cradle. 'American incunabula', therefore, are books printed in the United States before 1701 (compared with the terminal date of 1501 for European incunabula). This terminology has the advantage for the collector of providing a specific area to explore, a known harvest to reap. For some countries there are thoroughly researched bibliographies which will provide a reliable guide for the collector. The early imprints in Australia, for instance, are covered by Ferguson, and those in America are described by Evans. (Details of these books and of other useful bibliographies will be found in the Further Reading section, pp.152–5.)

The first book printed in a new land is always greatly prized, and it is nearly always extremely rare. The only known copy of the first book printed in the Philippines (dated 1593), for instance, was discovered only recently by an American dealer in a Paris bookshop. Printing in what is now the United States of America was not achieved until surprisingly late: the 'Bay Psalm Book', printed at Cambridge, Massachusetts, in 1640, an unpretentious little book of great rarity, is the first surviving book. Its almost iconic importance as the beginning of printing in such a powerful and literate nation has given it a status for collectors equivalent to that of the Gutenberg Bible. Intriguingly, we know that a sheet called 'The

The Whole Booke of Psalmes, [Cambridge, Massachusetts, printed by Stephen Daye], 1640.

The 'Bay Psalm Book' was the first book of any size printed in what has become the United States of America. Its title page does not say where it was printed, and a copy could be lying undiscovered in an American library or bookshop, waiting for a sharp pair of eyes to identify it.

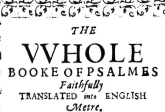

Arthur Phillip, *The Voyage of Governor Phillip to Botany Bay*, London, 1790.

Phillip's book relates the story of the first penal settlement in Australia, and has handsome illustrations of the aboriginal natives the settlers found there.

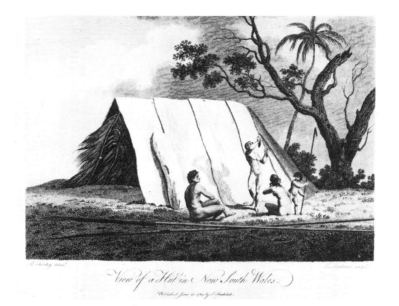

View of a Hut in New South Wales.

Freeman's Oath', and two little almanacs, were printed before the Bay Psalm Book at the same press, but no copies have been discovered. Unfortunately for the modern collector much of the early printed material from the most advanced countries is now in museums and great public libraries, and copies on the market are both rare and extremely expensive. But a similar approach can be applied to the emerging countries of Africa, whose printing history has remained unexplored by collectors and whose early printed productions are likely to be cheap. Alternatively, instead of hunting only the 'big game' of the first presses the collector could concentrate on the spread of printing in the early years of the new country.

Printing in a country is, however, only one way of approaching its literature: the first books about that land, or early maps and representations of it in books, or significant books and manuscripts in its history, may also be grist to the collector's mill. Books about discoveries are perhaps the most popular, ranging from the early editions of Columbus's letter to Ferdinand and Isabella announcing the result of his voyage, to accounts of the Pacific exploration in the eighteenth century. The Columbus letter is hopelessly rare, and most of the sixteenth-century books which so much as mention America are expensive, though not always actually scarce. The recent interest in the history of the American Indians has made books about the original natives especially sought-after, and the prices have risen accordingly. More within the range of the ordinary pocket are books on the series of voyages to the Pacific Ocean made by English, Dutch and French explorers in the eighteenth and nineteenth centuries. The better illustrated, such as the accounts of expeditions by Jean-François de la Pérouse (1797) and Captain James Cook, are relatively costly, but early (not necessarily first) editions of works on less important voyages—such as that of William Dampier

(1699–1703) or A. F. J. de Fréville (1774)—can be found for as little as £150.

The original accounts of Captain Cook's three voyages, published in the 1770s, are perhaps the most splendid monuments to great original discoveries ever printed. Particularly important was his second voyage, on which many new islands were named, but it was on his first voyage that Cook made his principal discoveries in Australia and New Zealand. The narrative of the first voyage (1768–71) was published in 1771, the second (1772–5) in 1777. The account of the last, tragic, voyage on which Cook was killed at Hawaii in 1779 was published in 1784. Each of these accounts can fetch between £500 and £1,000 at auction (more for good copies, less when battered or incomplete). More symbolic, perhaps, is *The Voyage of Governor Phillip to Botany Bay* (1789), the account by Phillip himself of the establishment of the first penal colony in Australia: this is an attractive as well as significant production and although fairly common on the market it regularly sells for upwards of £1,000 at auction.

The foregoing may have given the impression that all the collectable books on voyages are only for the very rich. However, if the obvious routes for collectors appear to have been well covered, there remain many areas for the imaginative collector to explore, and these are often cheap as well as intellectually rewarding.

Important books and documents in the history of a country are another line for the collector to pursue. Most of us collected autographs of famous people when we were young, and extending this to collecting the signatures of historical people when we grow older is a natural instinct. We may go further, and wish to possess interesting or significant documents signed or written by famous people; and the effect on the market of this sort of collecting is that more appealing or more typical documents in the hand of a great figure are worth considerably more than mere formal letters or signatures cut out and pasted into an album. Printed books which record the history of a nation will also be attractive to collectors, and for American bibliophiles the history of the struggle for independence and the Civil War are especially fruitful ground for collections: books relating to these two important episodes are keenly sought. Autographs of the Presidents of the United States, or books connected with them, can form an interesting collection, and although some signatures are expensive there are plenty which are not. Good examples of the writing of the early and of the great Presidents (such as George Washington and John Quincy Adams) are usually expensive, and the signatures of most of the Signers of the Declaration of Independence (1776) are also valuable—especially that of the elusive Button Gwinnett of Georgia (who died in 1777), which has taken on a significance far exceeding its historical importance. More recent American historical figures are of less value, but it is impossible to give any firm price-guide since the value of any manuscript document is determined as much by its quality and interest as by the identity of its author.

National pride is obviously a great stimulus to collections such as these, yet the libraries formed on such principles are not merely chauvinist. Like almost any form of book collecting, they have more interesting origins and

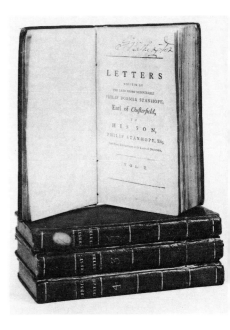

Philip Stanhope, Earl of Chesterfield, *Letters to his Son*, 4 volumes, London, 1775.

The third edition of Chesterfield's *Letters* is a common and inexpensive book—but if George Washington was the original owner, the price instantly accelerates. This set made $16,500 (£7,400) at auction in 1979.

RIGHT
David Roberts, *The Holy Land, Syria, Idumea, Arabia, Egypt and Nubia*, 6 volumes, 1842–9. Hand-coloured lithograph.

A few copies of Roberts's magnificent volumes of views were issued with the plates delicately hand-coloured and mounted on cards to resemble original watercolours. Their freshness and grandeur has made them popular (especially with Middle Eastern collectors) and very expensive.

uses than simply an obsession with a particular country. The John Carter Brown Library at Providence, Rhode Island, for instance, is now a major research library for historians of the United States, yet it too began as a personal collection of books on the early history of the nation; its Australian counterpart is the Mitchell Library at Sydney. In many other nations similar collections are being formed on a smaller scale, and whilst most of them will be dispersed some will be incorporated in larger libraries—and they will all lead to a greater appreciation of the history of the country through the printed word.

TRAVEL AND NATURAL HISTORY BOOKS

Books of voyages of exploration and discovery, travels, local topography and natural history are all about human curiosity, the desire to know more about the world in which we live and the races of men and the species of animals and plants with which we share it. Books about the landscape, architecture and costume of foreign parts widen our horizons and in a small way make us citizens of the world. Just as Napoleon, having conquered Egypt, commissioned one of the most ambitious of all travel books, the *Description de l'Égypte* (1808–28), with nearly a thousand large folio plates by the best artists of the day, including Redouté, Duhamel and Proudhon, so the eighteenth- and nineteenth-century travellers made sketches and bought books of aquatint or lithographed views, and the modern tourist takes photographs and buys glossy guidebooks.

Travel and natural history books usually have a serious purpose in communicating new knowledge, and as often as not the illustrations are as essential as the written descriptions—they may even be the sole medium of communication on occasion. But publishers have made the most of our Napoleonic curiosity and have made their books fit for the drawing-rooms of the rich as well as the libraries of the educated. The strong emotional—rather than historical or scholarly—appeal of bright colours and exotic subjects has made the market in these books both expensive and volatile.

Voyages and travels

Not surprisingly, accounts of voyages of discovery and exploration are popular among collectors, especially those whose homelands were discovered and written about after the beginning of the printing era. Although even those collectors with unlimited funds are unlikely to have a chance to buy a copy of the 'Columbus letter' of 1493—the printed version of Columbus's dispatch to the King of Spain announcing his discovery of America—there are, for almost any part of the New World, accounts of travels which invariably contributed something new to the knowledge of geography, natural history or ethnography of the day. The more important voyages are interesting to collect in depth: the official accounts of Captain Cook's three voyages (see p. 80) exist in numerous editions, and many of them demand as much attention as the first editions. But there were also many published accounts besides the 'official' ones: the first full account of the second voyage, for example, is the narrative of John Marra, a gunner's mate on the *Resolution* who had attempted to desert at Tahiti on 14 May 1774. His account was published in 1775, eighteen months before the official version, and it records many incidents omitted by Cook. There is a further surreptitious account written by another officer, who remains unidentified. Similarly, a large literature surrounds Captain William Bligh's ill-fated expedition to collect the bread-fruit native to Otaheite in order to introduce it into the West Indies. Bligh's own account is *A Narrative of the Mutiny* (1790), a rare book which has made as much as £1,000 at auction; but there are many other less expensive contemporary accounts not only of the mutiny but also of the extraordinary skill and bravery of Bligh's voyage of 4,000 miles in an open boat, and of the mutineers' life among the Otaheitans and their settlement of Pitcairn Island. It was a tale guaranteed to appeal to a generation entertained by Defoe and educated by Rousseau.

The accounts of voyages span the whole period of printed books and the early ones are predictably scarce and expensive. But they do mostly come on the market from time to time and it is not too daunting a challenge to collect at least some of the first-hand accounts of the great explorers whose names are well known—Amerigo Vespucci, for example, and William Dampier, André Thevet, Richard Hakluyt, Jean-François de la Pérouse, George Anson, George Vancouver and Louis de Bougainville. The first editions of the voyages of all of these except Thevet and Vespucci could have been bought in the last few years for between £500 and £3,000. André Thevet's *Les Singularitez de la France antarctique, autrement nomée Amérique* is very rare in the first edition of 1558, but other important early editions and translations turn up occasionally. Similarly, the earliest editions of Vespucci's four voyages, which were published in the first ten years of the sixteenth century, are very rare indeed, but as with the other major voyages numerous later editions and translations exist which can also be interesting to the collector for their influence on later explorers.

In the late eighteenth century and the nineteenth century, when the great continents were well known, voyages often had a more scientific character, typified by the voyage of the *Beagle* to South America and around the world from 1832 to 1836, under the command of Captain Robert Fitzroy, on which Darwin sailed as naturalist. The *Narrative of the Surveying Voyages of His Majesty's Ships Adventure and Beagle* was published in 1839 and the first volume, written by Darwin, was republished separately in the same year under the title *Journal of Researches*. It gives the details of Darwin's observations on the fauna of the Galapagos Islands and contains the germ of his Theory of Evolution. Many other nineteenth-century voyages gave rise to separate publications on natural history, ethnography, oceanography, astronomy and so forth: published accounts were numerous and widely read; and the modern collector can find the less lavishly produced versions for as little as twenty pounds.

A major area of travel collecting centres on the great atlases, the

Plate 1.

London, Published June 1826, by J.Cross, 18 Holborn, opposite Furnivals Inn.

Page 137.

AN EXPLORING PARTY IN NEW SOUTH WALES.

An OFFERING before CAP.ᵗ COOK, in the SANDWICH ISLANDS.

James Atkinson, *An Account of the State of Agriculture and Grazing in New South Wales*, London, 1826. Hand-coloured aquatint.

A good copy of this attractive and unusual book fetched A$7,500 (£5,000; U.S. $7,000) at Christie's in Australia in 1984.

James Cook and James King, *A Voyage to the Pacific Ocean in His Majesty's Ships the Resolution and Discovery*, 3 volumes and an atlas volume of plates, 1784. Engraved plate of Cook's reception at the Sandwich Islands.

Cook's 'Third Voyage', as this book is known, was his last: he was killed at Hawaii in 1779, and the narrative, with a splendid volume of engraved plates, was published posthumously.

LE PALAIS ET LA FORTERESSE DE JANINA, VUS DU LAC.
Un Turc et un jeune Grec.

Louis Dupré, *Voyage à Athènes et à Constantinople*, Paris, 1825.

The masterpiece of the French school of lithography: Dupré, a pupil of David, had travelled in Greece in 1819. A fine complete copy was sold at Christie's in 1975 for £6,500 ($14,430).

Renaissance versions of the Greek geographer Ptolemy and the new maps of Joannes Blaeu, Abraham Ortelius, Gerard Mercator and others. Because of the popularity of maps for framing, many atlases are being broken up, the maps coloured—often with no regard for authenticity—and sold for framing. (Avoid maps in bad condition or whose margins have been badly trimmed; beware also of brightly-coloured maps which may have been worked over by a modern colourist.) When they remain complete, atlases command very high prices as the book collector has to compete with the print-sellers who can spread the cost by selling the maps individually.

In parallel with these accounts of voyages were the numerous topographical works on countries in Europe and overseas, and the 'picturesque tours', costume books and travelogues. England held a unique position in publishing books of views with colour plates because of the skill with which English engravers and colourists imitated that peculiarly English medium, watercolour. William Daniell's *Voyage round Great Britain* (1814–25), with its subdued and often moody views of British coastal scenery, has always been a favourite; George Heriot's *Travels through the Canadas* (1807) contains twenty-six Canadian views; J. J. Middleton's *Grecian Remains in Italy* (1812) has large views of ancient Greek architecture; and Sir William Hamilton's *Campi Phlegraei* (1776) has dramatic black-bordered views of Vesuvius and its eruptions. These are frequently seen in the major British sale rooms, but the grandness of their execution has made them expensive properties.

Natural History

The earliest studies of natural history, like the earliest voyages of exploration, were undertaken with a strong practical purpose: the study of plants was primarily for medicinal use, and most of the earliest printed natural history books are herbals. Gradually, plants and animals began to be studied for their own sake and the books became more and more lavishly illustrated to cater for an increasing readership of dilettante naturalists.

The early herbals are all versions of the 'Herbal of Apuleius' (Rome, 1481?), the 'Latin Herbarius' (1484), printed by Peter Schoeffer, the 'German Herbarius' (1485), also printed by Schoeffer and the *Hortus Sanitatis* ('The Garden of Health', 1491), which also contains sections on fish, birds and other animals, minerals and general medicine. While the first editions of these works are of very great rarity, the derivative editions are sometimes found and have attractive although very stylized and primitive-looking woodcuts. For some reason the superb naturalism of the drawing from life seen in the works of the artists of this period (for example Dürer and Leonardo) was not applied to herbal illustrations until the woodcuts of the great *Herbarum vivae eicones* (Strasbourg, 1530–6) by Otto Brunfels and the *De historia stirpium* (Basle, 1542) by Leonhard Fuchs. From the point of view of illustration, these were the first modern botanical books, although their texts were still largely derived from the *Materia medica* of the herbalist Dioscorides, who lived in the middle of the first century AD. They were frequently translated and imitated and were

Leonhard Fuchs, *De historia stirpium*, Basle, 1542. Woodcut of the artists and woodcutter.

Fuchs was one of the fathers of modern botany and the author of one of the most beautiful modern herbals. A few copies were coloured, although the wiry outlines of the plants are perhaps more striking in uncoloured copies. The book is offered fairly regularly at auction, but as with all herbals good copies are rare and a fine uncoloured copy might make £5,000–6,000 ($6,250–7,500) at auction.

followed by a great succession of woodcut herbals by Charles de l'Écluse (known also as Carolus Clusius) and Rembert Dodoens, and in England by William Turner, John Gerarde and John Parkinson. These books are mostly now quite rare in their first editions, and they are still expensive in later editions since the blocks, used in edition after edition or even in different books, did not deteriorate significantly: prices are measured in thousands rather than hundreds of pounds.

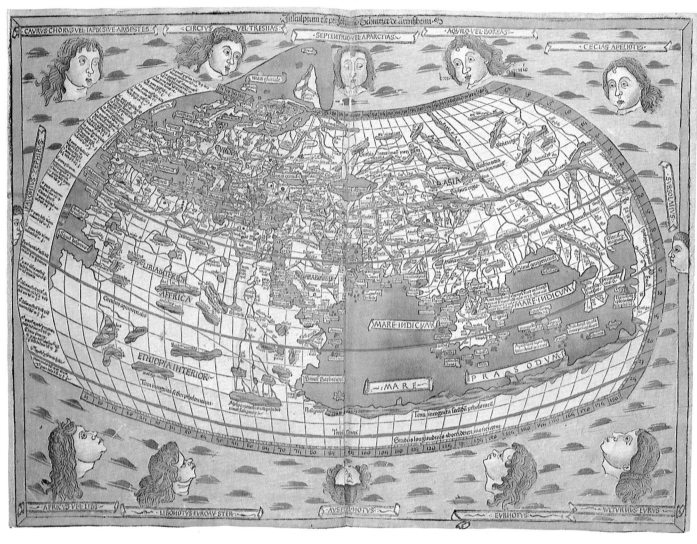

Claudius Ptolomaeus, *Cosmographia*, Ulm, 1486. Hand-coloured woodcut.

Early atlases show the world as traditionally understood by ancient geographers. In this map, printed and finely coloured by hand six years before Columbus, the world centres on Arabia, North Africa, Asia and Europe, with ten winds blowing from the corners of the earth.

Sir William Hamilton, *Campi Phlegraei*,
Naples, 1776–9. Hand-coloured aquatint.

Hamilton was a diplomat in Naples, with
enough leisure to indulge his passions for
volcanoes and ancient vases. One of the
classic colour plate books, his *Campi
Phlegraei*, is keenly collected and a fine
copy was sold for £14,300 ($17,300) in
1984.

Iris angusti-
folia alba.

Iris angustifo
lia variegata,
cæruleo alba
fl. pleno.

Iris bulbosa
angustifolia.

vulgaris
fl. pleno.

Iris lutea
odorata.

Johann Theodor de Bry, *Florilegium novum*, Oppenheim, 1612. Engraving.

A good example of the decorative florists' books which became more popular as horticulture improved. Separate prints can often be bought, though sadly they are often coloured up, and the colouring obscures the fine engraving.

Towards the end of the sixteenth century the art of botanical illustration became more sophisticated still, and around the turn of the century publishers began to replace woodcuts with finer copperplate engravings. Some of the most beautiful flower books were published at this time, artists and engravers vying with each other to produce the loveliest plates, just as the gardeners and florists competed to grow the most exotic and magnificent blooms. These are generally found un-coloured, though contemporary colourists (sometimes of great skill) were engaged by grander collectors to highlight their copies. Crispin de Passe's *Hortus floridus* of 1590, Basil Besler's *Hortus Eystettensis* (1613), and Theodore De Bry's *Florilegium novum* (1612–14) are examples. Sadly, they are out of reach of most collectors, but there are many lesser examples of fine work by their contemporaries and separate plates from these great works can often be bought, usually only in shops specializing in separate prints. The skill of the flower painters and engravers was not confined to decorative flower prints, and throughout the seventeenth century many serious botanical works were produced with outstanding plates, perhaps the highest point of botanical accuracy being reached with Nicolas Robert's *Recueil des plantes* (1672), with engravings by Abraham Bosse.

Thomas Bell, *A History of British Reptiles*, London, 1839. Wood engraving.

A good example of the high quality of illustration found in some of the less glamorous nineteenth-century books, in this case a book usually priced at £100 ($125) or less.

ANOURA.   RANIDÆ.

Genus, *Rana*, Linn.

Generic Character.—Skin smooth, hinder legs very long, formed for leaping ; the toes palmated. Teeth on the upper jaw, and on the palate.

Scientific botany was developing in this period as was zoology and mineralogy, and in the eighteenth century monographs and books describing the natural history of particular regions began to appear, such as Mark Catesby's celebrated *Natural History of Carolina* (1754), William Curtis's *Flora Londiniensis* (1777–98), and a host of smaller works on regional flora and fauna which are very interesting to collect and comparatively inexpensive. Botanical and natural history books were by now often issued with the plates already coloured. An interesting innovation at the end of the eighteenth century was the well-illustrated botanical periodical, the first and most famous of which was Curtis's *Botanical Magazine*, founded in 1787 and still being published regularly today. Here all the latest discoveries and hybrids are reported and illustrated along with details of cultivation and articles on scientific botany. Odd volumes of Curtis and the many other nineteenth-century magazines can often be found quite cheaply. Perhaps the most celebrated botanical books, however, are the works of P. J. Redouté, and many people will be familiar with his illustrations for *Les Roses* (Paris, 1817–24). But there are many smaller and equally beautiful botanical books by other artists of the late eighteenth and early nineteenth century—indeed this is one of the best periods for botanical illustration.

Zoological illustration, on the other hand, flourished throughout the whole of the nineteenth century. After the stiff bird-portraits of Redouté's contemporaries François Levaillant and Jean-Baptiste Audebert, Edward Lear's lifelike parrots in his *Illustrations of the Family of Psittacidae or Parrots* (1830–2), and his animal drawings in *Gleanings from the Menagerie at Knowsley Hall* (1846), paved the way for the well-known ornithological folios of John Gould—*The Birds of Great Britain*, *A Century of Birds from*

MACROCERCUS ARARAUNA.

Blue & Yellow Macaw

Edward Lear, *Illustrations of the Family of Psittacidae or Parrots*, London, 1832. Hand-coloured lithograph.

The prototype of the great Victorian colour plate bird books, strikingly lifelike in comparison with the work of former artists. This copy was sold at auction in London for £23,760 ($35,640) in 1983.

PLATE XLIV

Painted & Published as the Act directs by the Author G.Brookshaw.

George Brookshaw,
Pomona Britannica,
London, 1812. Hand-
coloured aquatint.

The grandest of
illustrated books on
fruit, with ninety large
folio plates. Imperfect
copies are a natural
target for dealers, who
break them and sell
the individual plates;
complete copies have
sold for over £30,000
($37,500).

the *Himalaya Mountains*, *The Birds of Asia*, *A Monograph of the Trochilidae, or Family of Humming Birds*, and so on. Lear himself contributed to some of these and taught Gould's wife Elizabeth to draw. All Gould's books are very expensive on today's market, though they are commoner than those of his predecessors—the cheapest sell in the £3,000–5,000 bracket.

Other Colour Plate Books

Besides travel and view books, and books on natural history, there are a number of other genres of colour plate books worth mentioning here. Rudolph Ackermann, for instance, an immigrant from Saxony who set up business in London in 1795, produced a series of semi-topographical works which were also vehicles for the fine hand-coloured aquatints which he published. Among the most famous are his 'Histories' of Westminster Abbey (1812) and of the universities of Oxford (1814) and Cambridge (1815); also his *Microcosm of London* (1808–10), which has aquatints of architecture and interiors by A. W. Pugin with figures added by Thomas Rowlandson. Also semi-topographical are the canal views in John Hassel's *Tour of the Grand Junction* (1819) and the railway views in Thomas Talbot Bury's *Coloured Views on the Liverpool and Manchester Railway* (1831). Apart from a few views in topographical works, architecture is rather poorly served by colour plates, and paintings too were more often reproduced in uncoloured engravings, generally in mezzotints, a medium which took colour badly but with which the skilful engraver could most successfully capture the nature of oils.

Adam Smith, *An Inquiry into the Nature and Causes of the Wealth of Nations*, 2 volumes, London, 1776.

Smith's great work is the bible of free-market economics. A surge of interest by businessmen, particularly in Japan, has made this a very expensive book in recent years: an immaculate copy in the original boards fetched £18,700 ($44,000) in 1980, but standard copies are sold by booksellers for prices ranging between $7,500 and $15,000 (£6,000–12,000).

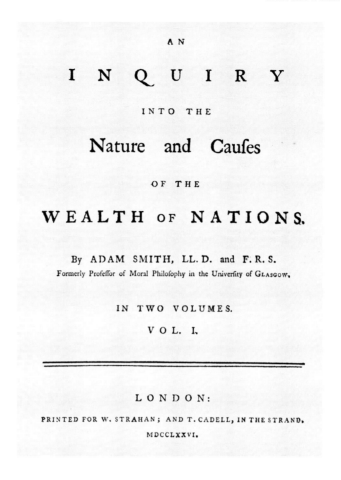

A N

I N Q U I R Y

INTO THE

Nature and Caufes

OF THE

WEALTH OF NATIONS.

By ADAM SMITH, LL. D. and F. R. S.
Formerly Profeffor of Moral Philofophy in the Univerfity of GLASGOW.

IN TWO VOLUMES.

VOL. I.

LONDON:

PRINTED FOR W. STRAHAN; AND T. CADELL, IN THE STRAND.
MDCCLXXVI.

THE HISTORY OF IDEAS

Collectors of rare books have most often concentrated on the literary aspects of their subject. Not until comparatively recently has another important feature of the history of the book received emphasis, namely the dissemination through the medium of print of theories concerning philosophy, or economics, or other social sciences which change the way we live and see ourselves. As with collecting scientific books, this area of collecting concentrates on the impact of a new idea on the world, and by possessing its first appearance in print the collector tries to possess the idea itself, and to illustrate its place in history.

The central place of Ancient Greek thinkers in western philosophy is largely ignored in collecting in this area. There is something unsatisfactory in pursuing first editions of writers who were dead centuries before the invention of printing, since it tells the collector more about the age in which the author was printed than about the author himself. Most early editions of classical authors are of little importance for their texts as these have since been greatly improved by modern scholarship. Collectors of philosophical works tend to limit themselves, therefore, to works conceived and written in the age of printing.

Frederick Ross, *Ruined Abbeys*, London, 1882. Colour-printed wood engraving.

A fine chromoxylograph printed in five colours from separate blocks. This is similar in appearance to a chromolithograph but is distinguishable by the shading achieved with closely spaced lines instead of the flat colours of the lithograph. (See also p.130.)

The first great effect produced by the printing presses was the growth of religious literature. It is no accident that the first printed book was a Bible. Without the spread of printing the Reformation could hardly have happened. Major collections have been made of early translations of the Bible, and of the works of the reformers such as Luther, Cranmer and Calvin, and also of the Counter-Reformation propagandists. Later religious books tend to be relatively inexpensive—perhaps they do not appeal to worldly collectors—but figures such as Wesley and Newman are seriously collected, as are the religious writings of major authors such as John Donne, or men of wide genius and influence like Thomas More or Blaise Pascal.

But philosophy in the sense of abstract speculation has tended to appeal less to collectors than the social and economic sciences, in which the human intellect has made more identifiable progress in the last five centuries. In particular, the developments in political philosophy, so profoundly important to the fate of millions, have inspired notable collections. Since the Italian humanists of the early Renaissance diverted attention away from God and focused on man himself, the striving towards a vision of a perfect society has resulted in a number of classic works, practical and impractical, honest and calculating. Whilst a number of these works are so severely practical as hardly to deserve the epithet 'ideological', the collector should remember that progress in the social sciences demands statistics as much as progress in the physical sciences, and that at certain periods in history the very collection of statistics was unusual enough to constitute an ideological advance in itself.

The examination of the human condition begins, inevitably, with the philosophy of the mind, and here the foundations of empirical philosophy were laid by an Englishman, John Locke (1632–1704), in his *Essay Concerning Humane Understanding* (1690). Locke was highly conscious of the contemporary advances in scientific thought—principally those of Isaac Newton and Robert Boyle—which also relied on the empiric method. He was not the first in his century to examine the workings of the mind and the nature of existence—one thinks naturally of the rationalist methods of Descartes—but it was Locke who may be said to have laid the foundation of the modern concept of the mind.

Locke's importance in this area of collecting is difficult to exaggerate, for he was also actively involved in politics in his role of adviser to the first Earl of Shaftesbury (who was virtually the first prime minister of England). As an advocate of religious liberty in an intolerant age, as an economist who helped to reform the coinage in the 1690s, and as an educationalist and theologian, he must also be seen as one of the founding fathers of modern liberal democracy. It was partly his philosophy which made possible the American revolution, since Jefferson was deeply influenced by him. 'Life, liberty and the pursuit of happiness' is Jefferson's combination of two of Locke's phrases, taken from different books.

The creation of a perfect society, one that is contented, free and immutable, has been a human dream ever since Plato's *Republic*. Yet more ingrained in modern mythology is the short work by Thomas More, first

DISCOURS
DE LA METHODE
Pour bien conduire fa raifon,& chercher
la verité dans les fciences.

PLUS

LA DIOPTRIQVE.
LES METEORES.
ET
LA GEOMETRIE.
Qui font des effais de cete METHODE.

A LEYDE
De l'Imprimerie de IAN MAIRE.
cIɔ Iɔ c XXXVII.
Auec Priuilege.

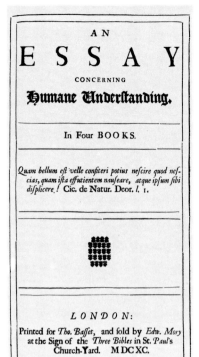

AN
ESSAY
CONCERNING
Humane Understanding.

In Four BOOKS.

*Quam bellum eft velle confiteri potius nefcire quod nef-
cias, quam ifta effutientem naufeare, atque ipfum fibi
difplicere.! Cic. de Natur. Deor. l. 1.*

LONDON:
Printed for *Tho. Baffet*, and fold by *Edw. Mory*
at the Sign of the *Three Bibles* in St. *Paul's*
Church-Yard. MDCXC.

René Descartes, *Discours de la méthode* [Discourse on Method], Leyden, 1637.

Cogito, ergo sum ('I think, therefore I am'): Descartes' famous maxim first appeared in this book, in which he attempted to construct an orderly universe based on logical thought.

John Locke, *An Essay Concerning Humane Understanding*, London, 1690.

The empirical investigations of John Locke (1632–1704) into the workings of the mind mark the beginning of a whole school of philosophy. Good copies of the first edition may be priced by dealers at £8,000 ($10,000) or more, depending on the state of the title page (this copy is the second issue). Locke made important changes in the second and subsequent editions, but because collectors will tend to seek the first, they only sell for a few hundred pounds or dollars.

Thomas More, *Utopia*, Louvain, 1516. Woodcut map of the island of Utopia.

More's short book on an ideal society has inspired hundreds of imitations, both optimistic and pessimistic. This copy of the first edition, the first to be sold at auction since 1944, reached the astonishing price of £81,000 in 1982. Later editions are also sought after for their attractive woodcuts by Hans Holbein.

printed in 1516, called *Utopia*. Written in Latin and only translated into English in the 1550s, it gave its name to a genre; and it has inspired hundreds of later imitations down to modern times, from Francis Bacon's *New Atlantis* (1624–9) and James Harrington's *Oceana* (1656) to William Morris's *News from Nowhere* (1890). Twentieth-century pessimism has inspired works ('dystopias') which hold up the mirror to a grim future that mankind may create for itself; the prime exemplars of this genre are Aldous Huxley's *Brave New World* (1931) and George Orwell's *Nineteen Eighty-four* (1949). The popularity of this genre for collectors is shown in the high prices paid for them—from £81,000 for a first edition of *Utopia* at a recent auction to prices between £50 and £100 for copies of the first edition of Orwell's book.

Obliquely relevant to such dreams and nightmares is Niccolò Machiavelli's *The Prince* ('Il Principe', Rome, 1532), in which a darkly ironic view of politics is proposed. Although Machiavelli's book is an antithesis to the ideal, his work dates from the beginnings of modern political philosophy and may be considered the starting-point for collections concentrating on the history of the subject.

But such early works are rare and expensive, and the eighteenth century remains the most fruitful area for the collector, partly for the very practical reason that the texts are more available for purchase, and partly because of the ferment of ideas which produced them. The Enlightenment encouraged the critical examination of man's place in society. The most notable book of this period, at once an expression of the spirit of the age and the foundation of its terminology, was Jean-Jacques Rousseau's *On the Social Contract* ('Du Contrat social', Amsterdam, 1762).

The question of man's natural rights was central to the political debate in France and America in the last decades of the century. The two classic works by Thomas Paine (1737–1809), *Common Sense* (1776) and *Rights of Man* (1791), dealt with both revolutions in a fresh and vigorous way. Both of these books, together with Edmund Burke's *Reflections on the Revolution in France* (1790, to which *Rights of Man* was the answer), were printed in large numbers and so are obtainable for quite modest sums; yet they remain among the most important and characteristic works of the age. The 1790s also saw the appearance of one of the great feminist books, Mary Wollstonecraft's *Vindication of the Rights of Woman* (1792) and also the publication of her husband William Godwin's *Enquiry Concerning Political Justice* (1793). These last two have recently become expensive books, their influence and status being increasingly realized by collectors.

Political philosophy seems to have depended more and more on the study of economics as the relationship between national contentment and good economic management has become more widely understood. There are few fields of human study in which one book stands so high as Adam Smith's *Inquiry into the Nature and Causes of the Wealth of Nations* (1776) does in economics. Smith's book has become the most celebrated work in the history of economic thought, and is consequently very expensive despite the fact that plenty of copies survive. It was not entirely original, but it was the first systematic treatise on political economy and it won a readership beyond the narrow world of academics. Quick acceptance by the British ruling classes of Smith's policies of free trade and libertarian economics has been suggested as a vital reason for Britain's supremacy in trade in the nineteenth century. In the middle of the twentieth century a similar dominance in economics was held by John Maynard Keynes (1883–1946), whose *General Theory of Employment, Interest and Money* (1936) is now a work sought after for collections concentrating on the economics of interventionist capitalism.

If free-market economics found their most eloquent expression in Adam Smith, the reaction that followed in the nineteenth century may be said to have culminated in the work of Karl Marx (1818–83). A long exile in London during the latter part of his life enabled Marx to work on his critique of capitalism, *Das Kapital*, though he was never to finish it. The first volume was published in Hamburg in 1867, the second and third being issued in 1885 and 1894, edited by Friedrich Engels from Marx's papers after his death. The first volume of *Das Kapital* is again an expensive book, whereas the further two volumes are usually seen as less vital and are consequently comparatively cheap. It was essentially as a hostile study of capitalism that Marx meant his work to be read, and it was only later that political constructions enabled it to be seen as the bible of socialism. Other revolutionaries and anarchists were, however, often as

REFLECTIONS

ON THE

REVOLUTION IN FRANCE,

AND ON THE

PROCEEDINGS IN CERTAIN SOCIETIES
IN LONDON

RELATIVE TO THAT EVENT.

IN A

LETTER

INTENDED TO HAVE BEEN SENT TO A GENTLEMAN
IN PARIS.

BY THE RIGHT HONOURABLE

EDMUND BURKE.

LONDON:
PRINTED FOR J. DODSLEY, IN PALL-MALL.
M.DCC.XC.

RIGHTS OF MAN:

BEING AN

ANSWER TO MR. BURKE's ATTACK

ON THE

FRENCH REVOLUTION.

BY

THOMAS PAINE,

SECRETARY FOR FOREIGN AFFAIRS TO CONGRESS IN THE
AMERICAN WAR,

AND

AUTHOR OF THE WORK INTITLED *COMMON SENSE.*

DUBLIN:

PRINTED FOR G. BURNET, R. CROSS, P. WOGAN, W. WILSON, P. BYRNE,
T. WILKINSON, W. GILBERT, P. HOEY, A. COLLES, H. COLBERT,
J. PARKER, J. CHARRURIER, J. BOYCE, R. MARCHBANK,
W. M'KENZIE, W. PORTER, C. BROWNE, T. HEERY,
B. DORNIN, J. JONES, J. MOORE, B. DUGDALE,
R. M. BUTLER, W. CORBET, A. GRUEBER,
W. JONES, H. FITZPATRICK, G. DRAPER,
R. WHITE, J. ARCHER, J. MILLIKIN,
R. M'ALLISTER, J. RICE,
R. CROSTHWAITE, P. MOORE
AND T. JACKSON.

M,DCC,XCI.

Edmund Burke, *Reflections on the Revolution in France*, London, 1790.

Thomas Paine, *Rights of Man*, Dublin, 1791.

The French Revolution inspired many books of polemic, but none was more famous than Burke's *Reflections* and Paine's *Rights of Man*. The horrified reaction of Burke to the revolutionary excesses in Paris typified the attitudes of British liberals who had previously welcomed the downfall of monarchy. Paine's widely circulated reply, which the British government tried to suppress, stated the fundamental principles of human rights. Many editions were published in 1791 alone; the Dublin reprint is illustrated here.

Das Kapital.

Kritik der politischen Oekonomie.

Von

Karl Marx.

Erster Band.

Buch I: Der Produktionsprocess des Kapitals.

Das Recht der Uebersetzung wird vorbehalten.

Hamburg

Verlag von Otto Meissner.

1867.

New-York: L. W. Schmidt. 24 Barclay-Street.

THE
GENERAL THEORY
OF
EMPLOYMENT INTEREST
AND MONEY

BY

JOHN MAYNARD KEYNES

FELLOW OF KING'S COLLEGE, CAMBRIDGE

MACMILLAN AND CO., LIMITED
ST. MARTIN'S STREET, LONDON
1936

Karl Marx, *Das Kapital* [Capital], volume 1, Hamburg, 1867.

The first volume of the theoretical foundation of Marxism, subtitled 'A critique of political economy', is a harmless-looking book, but its rarity and profound implications have made it an expensive commodity.

John Maynard Keynes, *The General Theory of Employment, Interest and Money*, London, 1936.

The interventionist economics of Keynes were profoundly influential in the years after the Second World War. His most important contribution to monetary and employment theory, published in 1936, is a common book but its significance has prompted collectors to pay comparatively high prices for it in recent years.

powerful in their influence as Marx himself. His friend Engels (with whom he wrote *The Communist Manifesto*, 1848), and also Ferdinand Lassalle (*System der erworbenen Rechte*, 'System of Acquired Rights', 1861), and Karl Rodbertus all wrote works which underpin twentieth-century socialist philosophy. In fact socialism, as one of the most original of nineteenth-century political philosophies, deserves study by the collector as a fascinating historical field with direct relevance to our modern condition.

In Britain, however, socialism largely failed to take on the radical appearance of the continental philosophy and it found a welcome at once more and less practical than elsewhere. Whilst for some writers—William Morris and H. G. Wells, for example—future socialism took on an almost utopian aspect, more empirical philosophers had already evolved the doctrine of utilitarianism. Jeremy Bentham (1748–1832), James Mill (1773–1836) and his son John Stuart Mill (1806–73) may be seen as the principal figures in this intensely practical philosophy, where 'the greatest good of the greatest number' was the declared aim. Bentham's most sought-after works are perhaps his *Introduction to the Principles of Morals and Legislation* (1789) and *A Fragment on Government* (1776); J. S.

Mill's *On Liberty* (1859) and *Principles of Political Economy* (1848) are also seen as important developments in practical philosophy. The mill-owner Robert Owen also published influential works on his industrial experiments; *A New View of Society* (1813–16) is especially valuable but other pamphlets may be found at more modest prices, as are many of the works of the Utilitarians.

The nineteenth century also saw the emergence of a more scientific approach to the social sciences. Demographic statistics of a sort had always been collected, though in a somewhat half-hearted manner, and one of the first critical analyses of the trends of births and deaths is the rare work by John Graunt, *Natural and Political Observations* (1661). But it was not until the upsurge of interest in such matters at the end of the eighteenth century, among the effects of which was the institution of the first national census in Britain in 1801, that a serious debate over the nature of population growth took place. The principal figure here was Thomas Robert Malthus (1766–1834), whose *Essay on Population* (1798, substantially revised in 1803) is now a rare and highly priced book. Despite the fact that Malthus's opponents found his pessimistic arguments difficult to answer, the progress of the Industrial Revolution and its effects on population actually tended to suggest his potentially authoritarian view of society was misguided.

If Malthus's work focused interest on the population question, other

THE BAKED POTATO MAN.
"Baked 'taturs! All 'ot, all 'ot!"
[*From a Daguerreotype by* Beard.]

ABOVE
Henry Mayhew, *London Labour and the London Poor*, 2 volumes, London, 1851–2. Wood-engraving from a daguerreotype.

Mayhew recorded the experiences of the new urban poor in their own words and illustrated them from photographs in a new kind of social reporting. The interviews make fascinating reading, and early editions (the book was reprinted in 1861–2) sell for around £100 ($125).

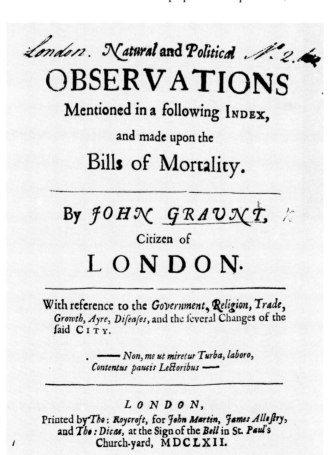

London. *Natural* and *Political* N° 2.

OBSERVATIONS

Mentioned in a following INDEX,

and made upon the

Bills of Mortality.

By *JOHN GRAUNT*,

Citizen of

LONDON.

With reference to the *Government*, *Religion*, *Trade*, *Growth*, *Ayre*, *Diseases*, and the several Changes of the said CITY.

—— *Non, me ut miretur Turba, laboro,
Contentus paucis Lectoribus* ——

LONDON,
Printed by *Tho*: *Roycroft*, for *John Martin*, *James Allestry*,
and *Tho*: *Dicas*, at the Sign of the *Bell* in St. *Paul's*
Church-yard, MDCLXII.

John Graunt, *Natural and Political Observations*, London, 1662.

Graunt's book introduced the practice of recording social and medical phenomena in the form of statistics. The first edition fetches in excess of £2,500 ($3,250) at auction, but four further seventeenth-century editions can sell for as little as £200 ($250).

students of society looked in more detail at the effects of urbanization. Henry Mayhew's *London Labour and the London Poor* (1851–2) is a searching and still highly readable account of the way the city's poor made their living. Later social scientists such as Seebohm Rowntree (1871–1954) are only now beginning to be appreciated by the book collector. Yet the progress of the social conscience is surely one of the major changes in the practical philosophy of most western people: in Britain it resulted in the welfare state after 1945 and in other countries in less stratified but broadly similar systems. This recent and profound alteration may merit investigation from the collector no less than the progress of economics itself, for if we acknowledge the history of ideas as an important subject for study, it is because of the practical effects of those ideas on the way we live now.

FINE BINDINGS

Eusebius, *Historia ecclesiastica*, Hagenau, 1506. Brown leather, blind tooled sides, brass clasps, *c.*1506.

A rare example of a binding by the 'Caxton binder'—so called because he worked for Caxton and for Caxton's successor, Wynkyn de Worde, in Westminster. The names of very few early binders are known, and modern scholars have given them names based on their styles or patrons.

The 'binding' of a book—strictly speaking the sewing, boards and outer coverings—evolved to hold together and protect the leaves of manuscript codices and printed books, which until recently were expensive articles expected to last for generations. Now that printing and paper are relatively cheap, and we are expected to consume rather than conserve, new books need no longer be so carefully protected with durable bindings. In the past bookbinding was a craft with a very practical purpose, and most bindings were made primarily for use, although they almost always displayed a craftsman's natural sense of design and taste for embellishment. The outer covering of the binding, of whatever material it is made, provides an obvious surface for decoration, and some books have always been lavishly ornamented, not only with gold tooling on leather but with chased or sculptured gold and silver, carved ivory, jewels and embroidery.

The history of fine bindings is also the history of bibliophily, for fine bindings are those executed for wealthy book lovers, or for presentation to those with influence. It is no accident that one of the greatest of early book collectors, Jean Grolier, gave his name to a style of binding as well as to a distinguished club for book collectors, the Grolier Club in New York. Bookbindings were normally executed to order and until the development of publishers' boards and cloth-covered bindings in the eighteenth and nineteenth centuries respectively the printer or publisher would not ordinarily have the books bound before they left his premises. Books were distributed unbound in folded sheets and the customer could either buy them in this form to take to his own binder or ask the bookseller to have them bound for him in a standard style. Quite often, too, the bookseller would have a small batch of ready-bound books for sale over the counter. Most book buyers would be quite satisfied with these 'trade bindings' but a few wanted something more special and would commission the bookbinder to execute a binding in a more expensive material, often morocco leather rather than calf, and would ask for it to be richly decorated with gold tooling, or with their arms in gilt on the covers. It is these special bindings that are now collected as 'fine bindings'. There is not an absolutely clear distinction between the two: 'trade bindings' are sometimes also 'fine bindings' (many bibles, for example, and other devotional works were bound for booksellers in a very elaborate style for retail) and the distinction is not really important. What the collector of fine bindings is essentially concerned with is the quality of design and execution. Of course really fine bindings have been rare and expensive from the first, and consequently the best can be priced in tens of thousands of pounds; but minor examples of good workmanship from, say, the English Restoration or the French eighteenth century can be found for as little as one or two hundred pounds; and damaged bindings, avoided by the most sophisticated collectors, can be bought for much less.

In the sixteenth century, bindings of wooden boards covered with white pigskin or brown calf were embellished with blindstamped decorations, either applied as single 'tools' or with 'rolls' (rolling tools engraved with a continuous design). Sometimes the rolls incorporated portraits of patrons, or pictures of saints, and many have been traced from one binding to another so that the work of a particular binder's shop can be established. In the fifteenth and into the sixteenth century, large books were often stored on their sides—on shelves or in chests—and in addition to this blindstamped decoration, the bindings were often provided with brass clasps to hold them shut and bosses on the sides to protect the leather from being scuffed when stored in this rudimentary and unsatisfactory fashion.

Gold-tooled bindings, which are what interest collectors of fine bindings most, were executed in Italy and France from the first years of the sixteenth century, and in England from rather later in the century. The decorations are built up from a large number of small individual tools so that an infinite variety of design was possible. In English shops, most of the individual craftsmen's names are unknown to us, but as with the blindstamped bindings the tools can usually be identified so that the work of different craftsmen may be distinguished and characterized stylistically: unknown binders have thus been dubbed with names such as 'Queen's Binder A' or 'the Small Carnation Binder'. Traditionally, collectors have sought out the most richly decorated, specially commissioned bindings, but almost any well-executed binding from medieval times to the present day is an attractive artefact, and it would often have been made by the same craftsmen who were commissioned to produce the finest work.

It may be said that the book market has always divided into two sorts of collectors: at one end of the scale the majority, whose primary concern is the text, or at any rate the interior of the book; at the other the collectors who have little interest in the content and will pay a high premium for the most lavishly decorated bindings, especially when these can be assigned to known craftsmen. These two styles of collecting, however, leave a wealth of secondary but nevertheless attractive and interesting gold-tooled bindings relatively underpriced.

The bindings executed for Jean Grolier (1479–1566) by various bookbinders, mostly in Paris, are immediately recognizable by their

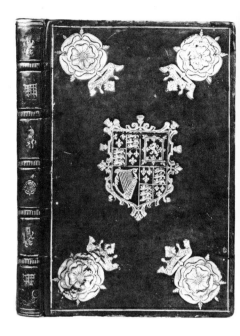

Themistius, *Opera*, Venice, 1534. English calf, gold-tooled, with the arms of Henry Prince of Wales.

Bound originally for Thomas Cranmer, Archbishop of Canterbury (1489–1556), this was acquired in 1609 by Henry Prince of Wales (1594–1612), eldest son of James I, who had his own arms added in the centre. Sold at Christie's in 1980 for £3,850 ($9,600).

OPPOSITE
Henry Noel Humphreys, *The Illuminated Calendar*, 1845. Gold-blocked and hand-painted paper-covered boards, designed by Noel Humphreys.

An especially gaudy Victorian binding. These bindings are not usually expensive, but are hard to find in such splendid condition.

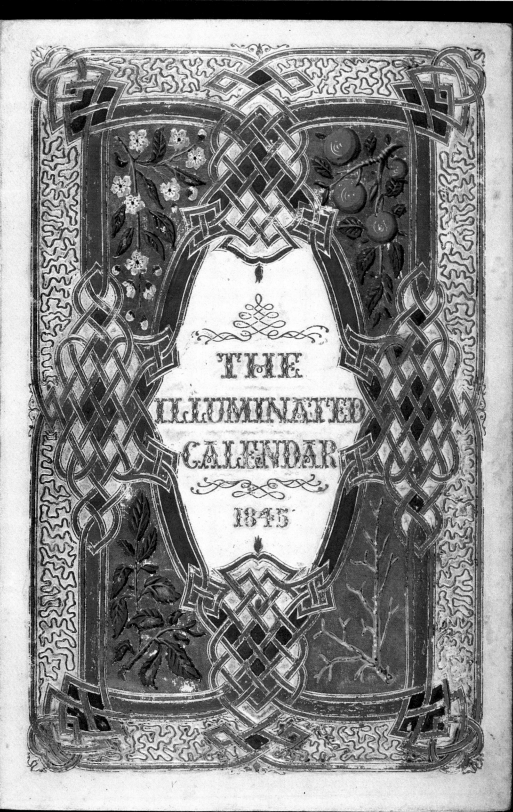

THE
ILLUMINATED
CALENDAR
1845

elaborate and characteristically Renaissance-style decoration of interlaced strapwork with the title in gilt letters on the upper cover and the words *Io. Grolierii et amicorum* ('[the book of] Jean Grolier and his friends'). Grolier amassed a good-sized library which was later widely dispersed and these beautifully bound volumes have always been keenly pursued by collectors: a few still surface in the salerooms from time to time, but most are in the care of the large public libraries.

Many gold-tooled bindings produced in the late sixteenth century were very richly tooled with the decoration covering the whole available surface (the so-called 'fanfare' style), but this fashion had only a brief vogue with the most discerning bibliophiles. The bindings executed for Jacques-Auguste de Thou (1553–1617), after Grolier the best-known French book-collector, illustrate phases in his collecting: following his first marriage in 1587, for instance, he seems to have tired of the ornate bindings which he had commissioned earlier and now required elegant and restrained bindings. His binders were still using the best materials and worked with the best techniques, but almost all de Thou's later bindings have no more decoration than his arms on the sides and his monogram in the spine compartments. De Thou married twice more and various monograms and arms on his bindings distinguish his different wives. His large library has been widely dispersed, with many examples still in private collections; today's bibliophiles therefore have ample chance to secure a book bound for him for prices ranging upwards from £200—depending on the quality of the book itself. This style of binding remained popular with French collectors for generations and good copies of books in armorial bindings ('aux armes') in morocco are as much admired today as they were in the seventeenth century—especially in France, where they are almost *de rigueur* in a sophisticated collection.

In England, by contrast, a robust and often startlingly flamboyant style developed in the later sixteenth century, where owners' crests filled the side of the book, corner ornaments invaded the whole surface and all the tools were strongly drawn and deeply stamped into the leather. This somewhat crude style gave way in the second half of the seventeenth century to a gentler but no less vigorous tradition which produced some of the loveliest bindings of any country or period. Some craftsmen are known by name—Samuel Mearne, for example, working in London in the middle of the century, and Roger Bartlett in Oxford a little later—others are known only from their work, such as the 'Naval Binder'. Their work is characterized by rich fields of flowers and leaves, barely held in check by architectural panels and by abundant foliage spilling over broken pediments ('cottage roof style'). Perhaps they drew their inspiration from newly imported oriental carpets: certainly the effects are often similar.

If the English bindings of this period are perhaps the more adventurous, it is in France in the eighteenth century that binding design and execution reaches heights of sophistication unequalled before or since. The great French illustrated books of the period, in bindings by Nicolas-Denis Derome or Louis Douceur, are fitting monuments to the departed glories of the French court. 'He who has not lived before the

Sulpicius Severus, *Historiae sacrae*, Cologne, 1573. Contemporary French red morocco, gold-tooled.

A plain but handsome binding executed for the celebrated French book collector Jacques-Auguste de Thou. Sold at Christie's in 1984 for £432 ($600).

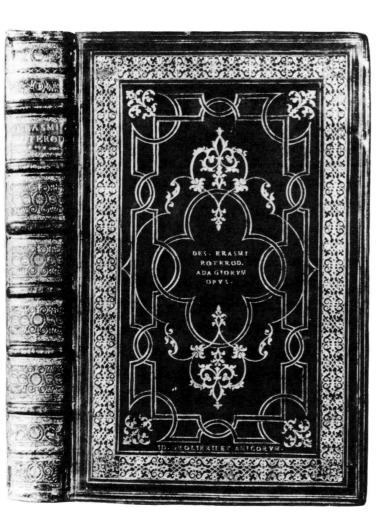 

Desiderius Erasmus *Adagia* [Proverbs], Basle, 1520. Bound for Jean Grolier in turkey leather, gold-tooled.

A fine Grolier binding, with the characteristic interlaced strapwork. Similar bindings do very occasionally come on the market, and they fetch high prices.

F. La Mothe Le Vayer, *Notitia historicorum selectorum*, Oxford, 1678. Bound in turkey leather by Roger Bartlett, gold-tooled, *c*.1678.

A characteristically ebullient binding by the Oxford binder Roger Bartlett. Binding history is still being elucidated, and Bartlett's work is gradually being identified in private collections and in the libraries of Oxford colleges.

revolution has not known the sweetness of life' wrote Talleyrand, and it is in these compact, delicate bindings, as personal as snuff-boxes and perhaps bound for a queen or a royal mistress, that one catches the full flavour of the *ancien régime*.

Binding styles sometimes follow contemporary trends in the decorative arts and sometimes go their own way. The brash rococo bindings of James Scott of Edinburgh and his few imitators form a somewhat unexpected, and practically isolated, episode in bindings of the later eighteenth century. More to be expected are the neo-classical bindings from the end of the eighteenth century (one or two actually designed by Robert Adam) which are typified by the famous 'Edwards of Halifax' bindings. James Edwards patented in 1785 a method of decorating vellum bindings in which delicate pen and wash drawings were executed on the underside of the vellum, which was then made transparent before being used to cover the book in the usual way; it was then further embellished with an array of urns, lyres and so forth. Bindings from the Edwards of Halifax shop are almost never 'signed' (that is, with the name of the binder discreetly

A selection of books, mostly in French armorial bindings, from the library at Chatsworth; sold at Christie's in 1981. The arms of certain collectors are recognizable: Madame de Pompadour's three castles at the top in the centre, the banded arms of Comte d'Hoym on the large volume at the extreme right of the third shelf down, and the chevron of Jacques-Auguste de Thou in the centre of the same shelf. Fine books from country house or other distinguished private collections excite strong competition in the auction rooms.

Heures imprimées par l'ordre de monseigneur l'archevêque de Paris, Paris, 1736.

An extraordinarily fine binding of cream morocco, inlaid with red and olive moroccos, enamelled in red and blue, richly gilt and with the arms of Louis XV of France in the centre. Such bindings have been kept in special protective boxes since they were made, and were always intended as exhibition pieces.

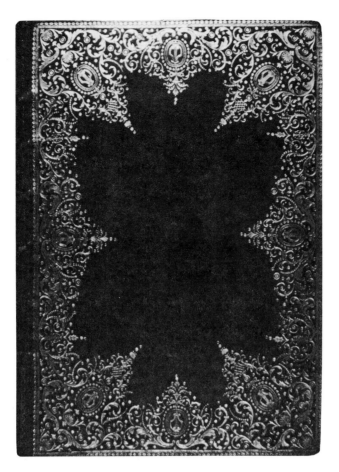

Les Grandes Croniques de France, 1493. French crimson morocco, gold-tooled, c.1770.

A binding by Nicolas-Denis Derome, called 'Derome le jeune', about 1770. This was a much imitated style, but Derome is held to have been the greatest of his age.

BELOW

Horace, *Opera*, London, 1820. Publisher's cloth, with printed paper label. 92×53 mm. ($3\frac{1}{2} \times 2$ in.)

William Pickering's miniature edition of Horace was the first book to be issued by a publisher in a standard cloth binding. This is now normal practice for publishers of 'hardback' books throughout the world.

tooled inside, or with a printed label), and since there were imitators of the new style, collectors should not suppose that every such binding comes from this workshop. A genuine, fully documented binding by Edwards will fetch several thousand pounds at auction; an unassigned binding, or work by an imitator may be found for a hundred pounds or even less, depending on the value of the book it covers.

Gold-blocked publishers' bindings began to be produced around 1830 and for the rest of the century publishers' bindings of brightly coloured cloth decorated with gold, blindstamping or colours (often combined) kept pace with the blooming of the decorative arts in the nineteenth century. In addition to the cloth bindings there were occasional uses of other materials, including morocco (there are some fine blindstamped examples designed by Owen Jones), wood, ivory and papier mâché, especially for the flourishing market for gift books which existed in the more affluent Victorian middle classes.

The relative merit of Victorian decorative art still provokes strong opinions among its adherents and detractors: for those who can appreciate the Victorian style, the bookbindings of the later nineteenth century offer a magnificent opportunity to collect some of the best examples fairly inexpensively. (Prices are mostly in tens rather than hundreds of pounds.)

James Beattie, *Essays*, Edinburgh, 1776. Crimson morocco by James Scott, gold-tooled.

Bound by James Scott of Edinburgh at the end of 1776 for presentation to King George III. Scott's use of classical motifs was a radical departure from the geometrical style of earlier Scottish binders and would have appealed to the patrons of Chippendale and Adam.

The challenge is not only to find the books—many are undocumented as bindings—but to find them in the best possible condition.

The tradition of gold-tooled leather bindings continued after the introduction of publishers' cloth bindings—leather bindings being much stronger and the desire for a luxury item unabated. Stylistically, hand-made leather bindings followed the Victorian decorative arts but not usually with the assurance of the publishers' bindings, which steal the show in the nineteenth century. The major exception to this are the superb and delicate bindings of T. J. Cobden-Sanderson at the Doves Bindery, which, it has been claimed, rescued the craft of bookbinding from half a century of purely imitative work. Bookbinding thus rescued has remained rather emasculated as a 'craft', not really knowing (like so many other skills) whether it is craft or a branch of fine art. Whilst the adventurous design of cloth bindings for mass-produced books, so prominent in the nineteenth century, has undergone an eclipse with the universal adoption of the dust-jacket and the prevalence of the paperback, individual craftsmen, inspired by the example of Cobden-Sanderson and his pupils, have continued to flourish. Modern collectors can have the satisfaction of commissioning new work for their books,

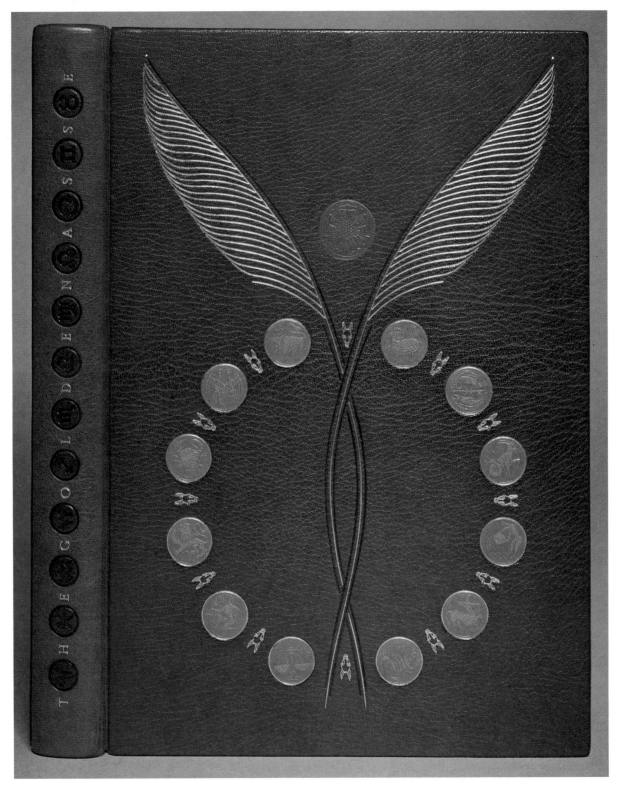

Lucius Apuleius, *The XI Bookes of the Golden Asse*, Ashendene Press, Chelsea, 1924.

This attractive binding by the English binder Roger Powell was executed in 1958 for an American collector, Philip C. Duschnes. The medallions inlaid into the cover and spine display the signs of the zodiac, and the feathers the ass's ears.

The Germ, London, 1850. Bound by the Doves Bindery under the direction of T. J. Cobden-Sanderson, olive morocco, gold-tooled, signed 'C. S. 1897'.

A nice example of Cobden-Sanderson's 'art nouveau' binding style, covering a copy of the short-lived Pre-Raphaelite magazine *The Germ*. This binding was sold by Christie's in 1979 for £1,320 ($2,700).

playing the creative patron in the twentieth century just as much as Grolier did in the sixteenth.

In the collecting of fine or even trade bindings, the condition is of great, even paramount, importance, since one is collecting not a text but an article. Like porcelain or furniture, the state of preservation of a binding is as much a factor in the object's rarity—and therefore price—as the skill or genius which went into its making. Demanding good condition in the bindings you buy is not mere faddishness but good sense and shrewd taste, whether the binding be the work of a known workman or by an anonymous journeyman.

3. The Book

PRINTING

Although the details of printing technique in the first fifty years after its invention are not fully understood, it is clear that it was not substantially different from the state of the art around 1500, which is well documented: the most remarkable fact is that the process did not change greatly for more than 300 years after that. In the early years of the nineteenth century printing was gradually mechanized, starting in the newspaper industry and following on much more slowly in book printing. An understanding of the technology of printing and its associated crafts in the hand press period will thus be useful to the collector anxious, as he should be, to know why books looked as they did up until the reign of Queen Victoria. Only a few new inventions, mostly the improvement or mechanization of old crafts, take the story to around 1900. The technology of modern printing is more complex and varied, but there are still some basic principles that will help towards an understanding of the book as a physical object.

We should really speak of *typographic* printing as the invention which revolutionized western culture: printing itself, that is the impression of a raised inked surface on paper or vellum, was well known in Gutenberg's day (see p.53). Typographic printing was an advance as it meant printing from movable type—single letters, or occasionally groups of letters, which had been cast on the ends of rectangular sticks of metal, usually an alloy of lead and tin. Groups of letters cast on one body ('ligatures') were much commoner in the early days, when printers were still trying to imitate manuscripts as closely as possible and therefore copied the professional scribes in the use of conventional abbreviations and joined-up letters. As type design gained its own identity, letter forms evolved which were better adapted to the basic principle of typography, so that the letters could be arranged in any combination, and only a few ligatures such as ff, fi and fl survived—though with computer typesetting (the method used in this book) even these have disappeared.

The individual pieces of type must be of exactly the same length so that they are evenly impressed in printing, and of the same height from top to

OPPOSITE
An eighteenth-century wooden or common press.

This press has been modified by the addition, in about 1800, of levers to increase the purchase on the screw.

An octavo forme. On the right are a mallet and a block of wood, used to tap down any raised letters before the wooden wedges or 'quoins' are driven up tight, using the mallet and the 'shooting stick' which is at the bottom right-hand corner of the photograph.

bottom of the letter (except for the ascending and descending letters such as d or g), as seen on the page, in order to form an even line. But they vary in width to accommodate wide letters like m and w as well as narrow ones like i, t and l. The mass production of identical or nearly identical and interchangeable castings was an extraordinary technical accomplishment in the fifteenth century; the process used represents one of the earliest examples of die-casting. The design of the letter is first engraved by hand on the end of a steel punch, which is then hardened in the fire and stamped into the block of soft copper — the die or 'matrix'. The matrix for a particular letter is fitted into a steel mould which is adjustable to different letter widths, and the 'types' (as the single letter are sometimes called) are cast one at a time. After the end of the fifteenth century typefounding became a specialist trade and most printers bought 'founts' of cast type, enough letters and spaces being supplied for the work on hand, the proportion of each letter varying according to the language to be set.

For hand setting, the type is kept by the printer in 'cases', shallow trays with separate compartments for all the letters and spaces. To set the type the compositor stands, or perches on a high stool, in front of a pair of cases (originally there was only one) propped one above the other on a wooden stand: the upper case holds the capitals and small capitals, the lower case the small letters. Reading off the copy he picks up the types one by one and puts the letters, upside down so that the line reads from left to right, into a 'composing stick', a small tray held in the left hand. When a few lines have been set up and the spacing adjusted to justify the right-hand margin, he transfers them to a flat surface to be made up into pages. The pages are surrounded by wooden blocks to create the blank margins and then wedged into an iron frame containing two, four, eight or more pages, ready for the press. This is the 'forme'. Two formes, an 'inner' and an 'outer' are prepared at once, one to print each side of the sheet. The pages

Composition. In the view at the top, two compositors are at work, picking out the letters and spaces and placing them in the composing stick as shown below. On the right a third man has imposed the forme and is tapping down any raised letters with a wooden mallet.

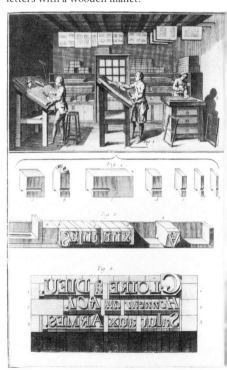

The Plantin-Moretus Museum in Antwerp.

The Plantin shop was the largest in Europe, having a maximum of 16 presses at work in 1574 and employing 56 workmen at its peak. Christopher Plantin's original shop was preserved by the family, who continued in business until the late nineteenth century, when the whole building was taken over to create a superb museum of printing in the sixteenth century.

Abraham van Werdt, A printing office in Nuremberg, c.1676. Woodcut.

An instructive view of the operations of the seventeenth-century printing shop, typical of all printing establishments in the hand press period. On the left compositors are at work setting the type from the copy fixed above their cases. In front of them the paper is being dampened prior to printing (the two trestles on which printed and unprinted sheets are shown is on the wrong side of the press). Pressmen worked in teams: the man on the left lays on and takes off the paper; the other inks the type with the ink balls (he is glancing at the printed sheet to see that his inking is even), runs the carriage into the press under the platen and pulls the bar to make the impression. Pulling was hard work and the men took turns, timed by the hourglass on the press.

are set out ('imposed') in the forme in a particular arrangement so that when the printed sheet is folded the pages of the book appear in the correct sequence.

Before the widespread use of cast iron in all kinds of machinery at the end of the eighteenth century, printing presses were made of wood and were of necessity massively constructed to withstand the great pressure needed to print several pages at once. Then in 1803 an English nobleman,

Charles, third Earl Stanhope, introduced the first iron hand press and others quickly followed, the iron press soon superseding the wooden or 'common' press. The method of printing on both kinds of press is the same. The forme of type, fixed face up on the bed of the press, is inked by one of the team of two pressmen using a pair of ink 'balls', stuffed leather pads with wooden handles held one in each hand and dabbed and rocked in the ink spread out on a board and then onto the type; later, gelatin-based rollers were used. The second pressman now lays the dampened paper onto a parchment-covered frame, the 'tympan', where it is held in position by sharp pins or 'points' projecting from the tympan and by another frame, the 'frisket', hinged to the tympan. He then folds the sandwich of tympan, paper and frisket down onto the type, slides the carriage on which the forme rests under the 'platen' (a flat block of wood, later made of iron) by means of a windlass and pulls the bar of the press which forces the platen down and presses the paper onto the type. For a clean impression, considerable force is necessary, and on wooden presses only enough pressure can be exerted to print half of the forme evenly: the carriage has to be repositioned and the bar pulled a second time. The carriage is then slid out and the printed sheet removed. In this way around 250 sheets an hour can be printed on one side — the speed depending more on the quality of the presswork than on the equipment used — by two pressmen taking turns at the light but skilled job of inking and the heavy work of pulling. Once all the copies of the sheet have been printed on one side, the pile of printed sheets is turned over, the forme changed for its pair and the process started again before the paper has dried out. The 'registration', that is the accurate alignment of the pages back to back, so important to the neat appearance of a finished book, is achieved by laying the paper on the tympan so that the points, which can be adjusted, go through the holes in the paper made when the first side was printed.

When both inner and outer formes have been printed they are returned to the compositor so that he can 'distribute' the type (that is, return each letter to its correct place in the cases). In a large printing house other sheets of the same book might be printed at the same time on other presses, but very often a whole book was printed on one press. In either case it was rare for more than a few formes to be imposed at any one time as type represented the printer's major capital expense and he did not want to stock more than he needed to keep the presses and pressmen continuously at work. The preliminaries — title page, preface and so on — were invariably printed last, as they still often are today.

This sequence of setting and printing has important implications in terms of reprints. Type metal was so expensive that even if a reprint was almost certainly going to be required quickly it was cheaper to distribute the type and reset the entire book than to keep the necessary quantity of type standing. In the late eighteenth century a way round this problem was finally found in a process called 'stereotyping'. A papier mâché mould of a page of standing type was made, and from it a thin metal plate was cast which was an exact replica of the original type and which could be duplicated any number of times. Before this invention, reprints were almost always new editions (from a bibliographical point of view), being

A Columbian press of 1822.

This is an iron press of the type that replaced the wooden presses of the first 350 years of printing history around 1800. The power is supplied by levers instead of a screw, the great eagle counterweight lifting the platen after each impression.

T. Kelly, A printing office *c*.1820 using a Columbian Press. Woodcut.

The Columbian press, in rather distorted perspective, shown in use. Note that the ink balls shown in the seventeenth-century printing office (p. 117) have been replaced by a roller.

fresh settings of the type with all the attendant possibilities of revision, correction and new error. When stereotyping became established, numerous impressions could be issued at different times, or simultaneously, in different countries. Which is then the true 'first edition' can be a nice question for bibliophiles.

Hand setting continued until towards the end of the nineteenth century, but the hand presses were gradually replaced by steam-powered and automatically fed printing machines with flat or cylindrical platens. Such presses were invented right at the beginning of the nineteenth century but because of the poor print quality of the early machines they were reserved for newspaper printing until the 1830s.

And so the last process to be mechanized was typesetting, and this came with the invention of keyboard-operated composing machines which held magazines of type ('cold metal'). These were followed by the much more successful 'hot metal' machines, which assembled matrices and automatically cast either solid lines of type (Linotype) or lines of single letters (Monotype). With Monotype, mistakes could be corrected in the usual way by removing and inserting individual letters. Generally speaking, Linotype was preferred for newspaper work and Monotype for books, although considerable use was made of Linotype setting for books in North America. Hot metal setting and printing on high speed cylinder platen presses has now largely been replaced, except for the highest quality work, by computer-controlled film or laser typesetting and printing by offset-lithography.

The success of Monotype technology, through the firm artistic leadership of the Monotype Corporation by the English designer Stanley Morison, played a major part in the development of book design in the

twentieth century. Under Morison's guidance a superb and previously unimagined range of typefaces was made available to typographers, ranging from adaptations of fifteenth-century Venetian types to new designs by Eric Gill. Filmsetting and laser-setting herald another revolution, but as yet this revolution seems to have gathered momentum without acquiring artistic direction: many modern books seem to have taken no account of the new design possibilities opened up by computer technology, though they may use to the full the mechanical advantages.

PAPER

Paper made from mashed linen rags, which is the earliest form of paper as we know it, began to be widely manufactured in Europe in the late thirteenth century. Before this, and indeed for long afterwards, books were written on vellum—untanned calves' skins, stretched and scraped to make a smooth writing surface. With the invention of printing, paper's potential for mass production recommended it as the only feasible material for large editions; vellum was only used in printing for a few de luxe copies of some books, as it was an expensive material. Indeed, it might be said that without the invention of paper, printing as a medium for effective communication would have been stillborn.

The most characteristic feature of paper of the hand press period is the pattern of lines which form an image of the paper mould. The mould is a rectangular sieve the size of the sheet of paper to be made, constructed with stout wires running parallel to the short edge at intervals of about 25mm. (1 inch), on which are supported much finer wires about a millimetre apart running parallel to the long edge: the widely spaced wires produce the 'chain lines' in the paper and the finer ones the 'wire lines'. The mould has a wooden frame like an empty picture frame, the 'deckle', fitted over it, making it into a shallow tray. To make a sheet of paper a quantity of sloppy pulp (made from linen rags mashed up in water) is scooped up from a vat with this tray. The papermaker gives the mould an expert shake to lock the fibres together as the water drains away between the wires of the mould, and the newly made sheet is turned out onto a piece of felt. Another piece of felt is laid on top of this, and a growing pile of alternate layers of felt and of fresh and still fragile paper is created.

The sheets are then pressed and dried, but as they are very porous, like blotting paper, they have to be 'sized'—that is, dipped into another vat, usually containing a solution of gelatin. After drying again and pressing, the paper is ready for printing, although for writing-paper the sheets need to be rolled or hammered smooth.

A sheet of hand-made printing paper is rectangular with feathery edges—deckle edges, caused by the pulp seeping under the deckle—and patterned all over with a grid of chain lines and wire lines. The paper may also be watermarked and show, especially when held up to the light, the paper-maker's mark, or a name and date, left in the paper as the image of fine wires attached to the mesh through which the water has drained.

Paper with chain lines and wire lines is known as 'laid' paper, and all paper was like this until the mid-eighteenth century. Then in about 1755 an English paper-maker, James Whatman the elder, made some paper for the printer John Baskerville of Birmingham on moulds made with a woven wire mesh. This was known as 'wove' paper, and was much more homogeneous than laid paper as it did not have the lines which Baskerville thought interfered with the purity of his typography. Wove paper was not made in quantity, however, for some years after Whatman made it for Baskerville.

Paper-making machines were invented at the beginning of the nineteenth century. In these the mould was not a flat sieve but a continuous belt of woven wire mesh, usually on a large drum. The paper pulp dribbled onto the moving belt or roller and was peeled off further along as a continuous web, which then passed through pressing and drying rollers, sizing vats and so forth. The web was cut into sheets—like the hand-made sheets but with only two deckle edges—for printing on hand presses and the early steam presses; large modern printing machines can print on both sides of the continuous web before it is cut and folded.

Most nineteenth-century machine-made paper was wove paper, although laid paper could be imitated and it was still preferred for writing paper and was used by printers with antiquarian tastes. The printer Thomas White often used machine-made laid or 'ribbed' paper (as it is more appropriately called when not made by hand) for William Pickering (1796–1854), who was significantly both an antiquarian bookseller and a publisher: the ribs on laid paper, which had been so painstakingly removed by technical advances, were in demand once again.

FOLDING AND GATHERING

The size and shape of the sheet of printing paper, and the way it is folded, together determine the size and shape of the book. Let us look at folding first. In a 'folio' (sometimes abbreviated to 2o) book the sheet is folded once only, with two pages of text printed together on each side of the sheet. The finished book will then be half the size of the sheet (or a little less if it is trimmed in binding). In 'quarto' (4to) books the paper is folded

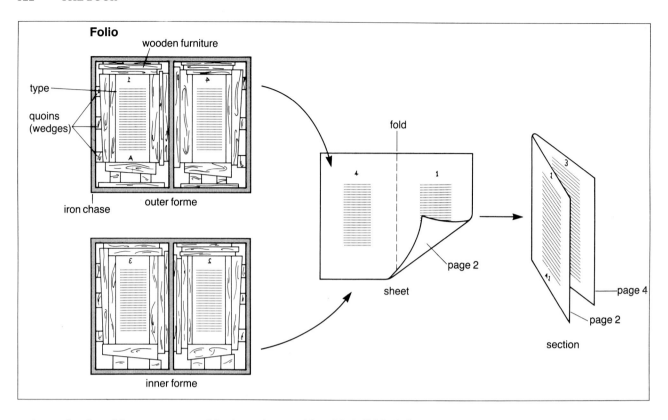

The arrangement of the pages of type (imposition) and folding sequence for folio, quarto and octavo sheets.

twice and printed four pages to a side; in an 'octavo' (8vo) it is folded three times and printed eight pages to a side. Thus when the same size of paper is used, folio, quarto, octavo, duodecimo, etc. are progressively smaller books. However, the actual size of the book is determined by the size of the original sheet of printing paper, thus a quarto printed on a small sheet of paper can be as large as an octavo printed on a larger sheet. So we must next consider the size and shape of the sheet.

The proportions of hand-made paper tended to be 1:1.25 or 4:5, squarer, that is, than the modern A sizes, which are so designed that each time the sheet is halved the proportions remain the same. (This means the proportion is $1:\sqrt{2}$, about 1:1.4.) The squarish shape of the hand-made sheet, on the other hand, means that when it is folded it becomes a tall narrow folio, then a squarish quarto and then a tall narrow octavo. Furthermore because the widely spaced chain lines in the paper run parallel to the short side of the sheet they run up and down a folio leaf, from side to side on a quarto, and up and down an octavo. Duodecimos can be folded in various ways to produce either arrangement of chain lines. The commonly used sizes of paper varied considerably from time to time and from place to place during the hand press period, so that, without a lot of specialist knowledge, attaching a name to the size of the paper in any one book is rather arbitrary. Thus a bookseller may describe a book as 'post 8vo', or 'imperial 4to', but generally he is using such designations loosely and they are more or less without meaning unless they are based on an accurate bibliography which describes copies that have not been cut

Quarto

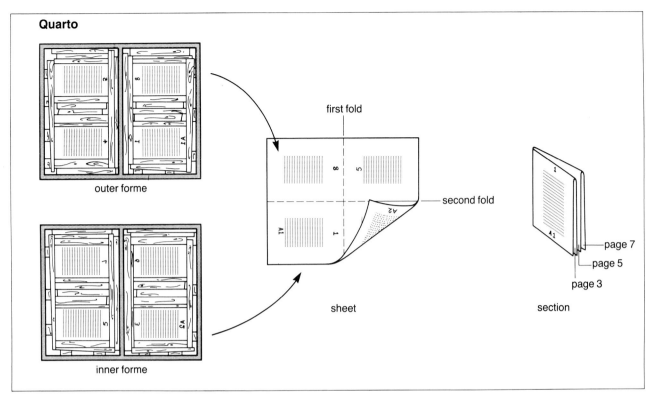

outer forme

inner forme

first fold

second fold

sheet

section

page 7
page 5
page 3

Octavo

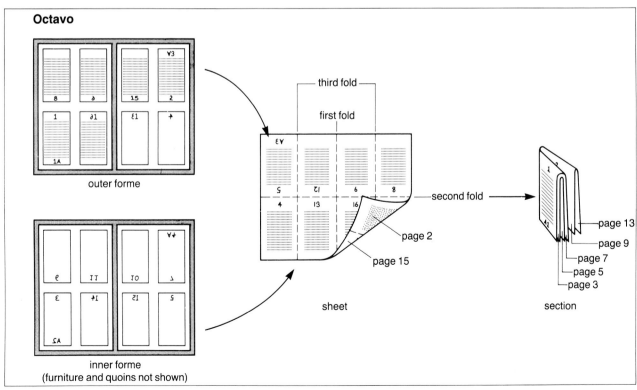

outer forme

inner forme
(furniture and quoins not shown)

third fold

first fold

second fold

sheet

section

page 2
page 15

page 13
page 9
page 7
page 5
page 3

down by the binder. However, at each period there was a fair degree of uniformity in the paper sizes most commonly used—a uniformity which increased with time, so the collector will soon know to expect a sixteenth-century folio to be about 30 × 20 cm. (12 × 8 in.) or an eighteenth-century quarto to be 28 × 22 cm. (11 × 8¾ in.), with other formats to match.

The folding of the sheets determines not only the shape of the book but also the imposition scheme and the construction of the book. For example, in an octavo the folded sheet produces, as we have seen, eight leaves forming a gathering or quire. The book is made up of a succession of these gatherings sewn together through the back fold. When the folded edges are trimmed off there will be four pairs of leaves joined at the back and tucked one inside the other. Folio books can be made in this way with a series of two-leaf gatherings ('bifolia'), or, to save sewing, two or three bifolia can be folded together, one inside the other, to make four- or six-leaf gatherings (technically described as 'folio in fours' or 'folio in sixes'). The printer usually inserts 'signatures', a series of letters or numbers, at the foot of the first few pages of each gathering to enable the bookbinder quickly to arrange the gatherings in the correct order, a process called 'collating'. Nowadays books are printed on presses which can print 16, 32, 64 or more pages at once and gatherings are larger, whether they are cut and glued for paperbacks or sewn in the traditional way.

The sequence of signatures intended to help the binder is useful to the collector as well, for it enables him to check if a book is complete by making his own 'collation' (the same term being used by both binder and bibliographer). It was common to sign the gatherings with the letters of the Latin alphabet (our 26 letters minus J, V and W), starting on the first page of the text with B. In the mind of the printer, A was reserved for the title page and preliminary matter, whether signed or not, which were usually printed after the text. Thus a typical eighteenth-century octavo might have the signature 'A' followed by 'B–Z', and we know immediately that the book should have $8 \times 23 = 184$ leaves or 368 pages, probably numbered i–xvi and 1–352: the bibliographer's formula for this is 'A^8 B–Z^8; pp. xvi, 352'. Of course there are endless variations of rather daunting complexity, and internal evidence of this sort is not an infallible guide to the correct make-up of any particular book; nevertheless it is often worth mastering the basic techniques of descriptive bibliography so as to be able to do a rough check, perhaps in a country bookshop, or to follow the description in a bibliography before it is too late to return the book to the auctioneer or dealer.

ILLUSTRATION AND PLATE-MAKING

The earliest book illustrations were printed from blocks of wood, a technique which may have preceded printing with movable type, although the impressions were probably made by rubbing the paper onto the block rather than by using a press. Woodblocks or woodcuts are made with small chisels, the white parts of the design being cut away to leave

Juliana Berners, *The Book of St. Albans*, London, 1496. Woodcut.

A rather simple style of woodcut (compare it with the woodcut done by Dürer a few years later, opposite page), showing particularly clearly in the river how the black lines are formed by chiselling out the wood in between.

Hroswitha, *Opera*, Nuremberg, 1501.
Woodcut.

A large woodcut by Albrecht Dürer,
much more sophisticated in technique
than the work being done in England at
the time, but still showing the restraints
of the medium in the shading.

Edward Lear, *A Book of Nonsense*,
London, 1863.

This illustration shows the facility with
which nineteenth-century wood
engravers could imitate pen drawing.
(See also the illustrations from books by
Mayhew and Bell on pp. 33, 102 and 91.)

There was an Old Man of Madras,   who rode on a cream-coloured ass;
But the length of its ears,   so promoted his fears,
That it killed that Old Man of Madras.

the lines to be printed in raised relief, much like the letters of printer's
type. Woodblocks could therefore be printed in exactly the same way as
the type and they were often combined in the same page, which allowed
great flexibility in the layout: the balanced composition of text and
illustrations in early book design has seldom been rivalled. Occasionally
illustrations were printed in two colours (from two separate blocks), the
results being known disingenuously as 'chiaroscuro' prints.

The early woodcuts were made on fruit-wood in the plank—that is
with the grain running at right angles to the printing surface. At the end of
the eighteenth century, when woodcut illustrations had almost disappeared in the face of competition from the finer copperplate engravings,
Thomas Bewick of Newcastle-upon-Tyne discovered that much finer
results could be obtained by engraving the design on the end grain of
close-grained timber, usually boxwood. Prints made from such blocks are
called wood-engravings, to distinguish them from the plank-grain
woodcuts of the earlier period, and the technique was used right through
the nineteenth century with amazing versatility and variety. Even large
newspaper illustrations were made in this way by jointing many smaller
blocks together: sometimes for speed a whole team of engravers worked
simultaneously on different sections of the picture before it was
assembled.

126

D. Diderot and J. le R. D'Alembert, *Encyclopédie*, Paris, 1769. Engraving of an engraving press.

In the centre of the picture a copper plate is being printed. Even without considerable leverage of the spokes the printer has to use all his weight to turn the press, such is the pressure needed to force the paper into the engraved lines on the plate. On the right the man at the back is inking a plate, while his colleague is wiping another so that the ink remains only in the grooves, and giving the blank parts a final polish with the palm of his hand.

Around the year 1600, copperplate engraving started to take over from woodcuts for finer work. In copperplate engraving the lines of the drawings are incised with a sharp-pointed 'burin' held against the palm of the hand and pushed across the surface of a polished copper plate. The printing process is quite different from the relief printing of type and woodcuts or wood-engravings. To print from a copper plate the ink is spread over the plate and then wiped off while being retained in the grooves cut by the burin. Dampened paper is then laid over the plate, and paper and plate are covered with a soft blanket and put through a press like a clothes-mangle which forces the paper into the lines to pick up the ink. Copperplate illustrations have to be printed in a separate operation from the text of the book. They can be printed on the same page as the text, after the text has been printed in the usual way, but this is quite difficult. Copperplate illustrations were therefore often printed on separate leaves, which were later bound in with the text sheets. An advantage of separate printing of text and plates is that the image is not spoiled during the impression of the type on the other side of the leaf.

Copper plates may be engraved in a number of different ways in addition to simple line engraving. In *etching* the plate is covered over with a thin layer of wax and the design drawn with a sharp point which removes a fine line of wax, exposing the copper underneath. The plate is then covered in an acid which eats into the copper thus exposed, making grooves which will hold the ink just like the lines engraved by the burin. In *aquatint engraving* the plate is covered with a porous coating through which the etching acid attacks the plate, producing a surface which prints as a grey tone; by stopping the action of the acid in certain areas a design can be built up of graded tones, usually with the outlines delineated by ordinary etching. Aquatint plates are ideal for hand colouring to imitate watercolours, and many colour plate books were made in this way. For *mezzotint engraving* the plate is first covered in tiny pits with a toothed rocker, so that when inked the plate cannot be wiped clean and prints as a solid black. The design is then created by hammering and burnishing the surface smooth again to produce a picture with an infinite gradation of tone from velvety black to white. This process is usually combined with

The Holy Bible, the first edition of the 'Authorised Version', 1611. Engraved title page.

Engraved title pages were common in the seventeenth century, and this is a particularly good example, showing the precision of line and shading that could be achieved. The lettering, engraved with the rest of the page, is based on pen-drawn letters. Later the precision of engraved lines was to give rise to the term 'copperplate script' for a very measured script.

ABOVE, RIGHT
Fabio Columna, *Phytobasanos*, 1592. Etching with border of printer's flowers.

A very early use of etching in natural history illustration. In etching the artist draws on a wax-coated copper plate, baring the surface of the plate to the etching acid. The lines are much more fluid than in ordinary engraving. The ornaments round the side of the plate are, confusingly, called 'flowers' and are used throughout printing history to decorate margins.

line engraving with the burin. In the last of the simple kinds of copperplate engraving, *stipple engraving*, tones are built up by making tiny dents in the plate as in mezzotint, but only where the design is to print. Plates engraved in this way were sometimes used in a kind of colour printing (called 'à la poupé'), in which the plate was inked with several colours at once in different parts of the design and printed at one impression; Redouté's great illustrations of flowers were made in this way, although in the best copies the prints were finished with water-colour, applied by hand. Since all these methods of engraving produce plates which are printed in the same way the different techniques can be used in combination, and the classification of prints is often uncertain. An important nineteenth-century innovation in engraving was the use of steel plates instead of copper plates, which made finer lines possible, giving more of an impression of continuous tone: it also allowed much longer print-runs before the plate became worn and the finer lines faded out.

The nineteenth century saw a proliferation of new techniques for printing illustrations but only two wholly new methods came into use which had any real impact and need concern us here. These are *lithography*, invented at the end of the previous century, and the various processes of photomechanical reproduction, which however eluded all inventors in any really economic form until the development of half-tone reproduction at the end of the century. Images produced directly from photographs without intermediate hand work did not begin to appear in books in large numbers until the turn of the century with *photogravure*, *halftones* and *photolithography*. Photogravure is a method of engraving

Rudolph Ackermann, *The History of the Abbey Church of St. Peter's Westminster*, 2 volumes, London, 1812.

The art of the aquatint reached its height in late eighteenth- and early nineteenth-century England, where its capacity to reproduce the effects of watercolour (when carefully hand-coloured by the publishers) was much admired. Rudolph Ackermann, an immigrant from Saxony, was the most popular and successful of the aquatint publishers, dealing mainly with topographical subjects.

photographic images onto copper or steel plates and it is used today for high-quality reproduction work and for both text and illustrations in high-volume printing such as magazines. Halftones are familiar to us today from their universal use in newspaper illustrations.

Lithography is a completely different printing process from those encountered so far. Generically this kind of printing is known as 'planographic' printing, because the image is printed from a flat surface and not from raised or incised lines. In lithography the design is drawn on the smooth surface of a block of porous limestone with greasy chalk or pencil and then fixed with dilute acid. To print the image the stone is dampened and inked with a roller: the oil-based ink is repelled by the water in the porous stone but sticks to the greasy chalk lines and is transferred to the paper with light pressure. Lithographs are almost invariably printed separately from the text of a book. The advantage of the lithographic process is that for the first time the artist's drawing was reproduced exactly, for he could himself draw on the stone. He did not have to rely either on the use of chisels and engraving tools, which imposed their own stylistic restraints, or on the intervention of professional engravers. Edward Lear (1812–88) was among the pioneers in England of the use of lithography in books with his *Illustrations of the Family of Psittacidae or Parrots* (1830–2), which marked a turning-point in natural history illustration, being the first book with really lifelike drawings of animals; it is the direct ancestor of John Gould's great folio books of bird illustrations (see pp.91–4).

Lear's plates were hand-coloured, but lithography was destined to revolutionize coloured illustrations in another way, as it became the basis of the first commercially successful form of colour printing. Book illustrations had been coloured by hand from the earliest days but until the eighteenth century this was mostly done individually and to order, either professionally or by the owners themselves. Then increasing prosperity and an interest in travel and natural history subjects created a market for large and expensive books with coloured plates, and whole editions were coloured for the publishers. The colourists, often children, worked from a set of key plates prepared by the artist and achieved a

Edward Young, *The Complaint, and the Consolation, or Night Thoughts*, illustrated by William Blake, 1797.

Blake's illustrations to Young's *Night Thoughts* are one of the most original and striking series of engraved plates ever produced. Blake's memorable marginal illustrations were created by the use of conventional engraved plates; in illustrating his own poems he used more complicated and personal means, printing and colouring each copy himself.

remarkable degree of uniformity from one copy of a book to the next; sometimes this was achieved by a production-line process in which one colourist would paint all the skies and other blues, the next all the greens, and so on. Even so, this was an expensive process and cheaper versions of the books were often sold with the plates uncoloured or only partially coloured. The original coloured copies command very much higher prices today than the uncoloured ones, and unscrupulous dealers sometimes have them coloured up and the unwary collector can easily be misled by such practices.

Various attempts were made at colour printing from one or more copper plates but the results either were too expensive, though very attractive, or could not compete in quality with hand-coloured plates. Sometimes, as for example in the books of Redouté mentioned above, the plates were partly printed in colour and then finished by hand.

Chromolithography was, obviously enough, the name given to the technique of printing coloured pictures from several different lithographic stones or plates, each supplying a different colour. The oil colours were gaudy and thick and there is no danger of confusing a chromolithograph with even the richly applied watercolour of Victorian hand-coloured books. Hand colouring was still preferred for the best and most expensive books, and the great Victorian folio travel and natural history books are mostly hand-coloured, but now the basis of the plate was a lithograph, rather than an engraving as it had been in the eighteenth century. An intermediate form was the tinted lithograph in which one, two or more tint stones were printed in combination with the black outline. Very subtle effects were obtained in this way, as seen for example in J. C. Bourne's *History and Description of the Great Western Railway* (1846). In David Roberts's *Holy Land* (1842–9), even more elaborate tint stones were used to produce the most evocative sunsets and interiors. Even so, de luxe copies of the book were sold with the plates fully hand-coloured over the tints.

Some very grand books were produced by chromolithography—Owen Jones's *Grammar of Ornament* (1856), for example—but it was chiefly used for smaller and cheaper books, which can be very attractive, and very Victorian in character. Colour printing from wood-engravings was also developed by a few printers in the nineteenth century and the prints are quite similar to chromolithographs. The chief exponent of this technique was the wood-engraver and printer Benjamin Fawcett of Driffield on Humberside. His plates are more delicate than most chromolithographs produced by his contemporaries: one of his best books is Frederick Ross's *Ruined Abbeys of Great Britain*, 1882 (see page 96).

BINDING

As we have seen, books are printed not on single leaves, but on large sheets of four, eight, twelve, sixteen or more pages. Each sheet is folded once, twice, three times or more, and the folded sheets are assembled to form a complete book, ready for sewing by the binder. The sewing-thread passes through the fold in the inner margin and round a series of thongs or cords running across the spine of the book. Early books were sewn onto leather thongs which were simply nailed into grooves cut into wooden—usually oak—boards, or laced through holes drilled in the edges of the boards. The book was then covered with leather, white pigskin or calf, glued either just over the spine leaving three quarters of the boards uncovered, or over the whole binding of cords and boards. These bindings were often elaborately blind-tooled (impressed with a decorative pattern, but without gilding or other decoration) and sometimes had leather or silk ties or brass clasps to hold the book shut. Often smaller books of this early period, mostly before about 1600, were sewn on to strips of vellum, which were threaded into a simple vellum cover without using any glue. These bindings are described as 'limp vellum', as opposed to 'vellum boards', a slightly later style of binding, in which the vellum covering was applied over pasteboard sides to which the cords were attached. Binding with vellum boards gradually replaced the use of pigskin and was common in Europe until well into the eighteenth century.

During the sixteenth century pasteboard sides replaced oak boards, and hemp or jute cords replaced the leather thongs which had a tendency to crack. At the end of the century saw-cuts were often made in the back of the book and the cords sunk in so that the sewing thread simply passed across them instead of having to be looped round. Sometimes in these bindings, especially the grander ones, sham raised bands were made on the leather covering the spine, to imitate the earlier style, but sawn-in cords never completely replaced raised cords.

John C. Bourne, *The History and Description of the Great Western Railway*, 1846. Tinted lithograph.

Tinted lithographs are printed from two stones, used one after the other. The first prints the drawing itself, which appears like a pencil or crayon drawing; the second, the tint stone, adds a tint which is like a watercolour wash. Highlights are produced by etching the tint stone to produce white areas which show up brightly against the surrounding tint, as for example the patch of sunlight behind the engine's funnel in this picture.

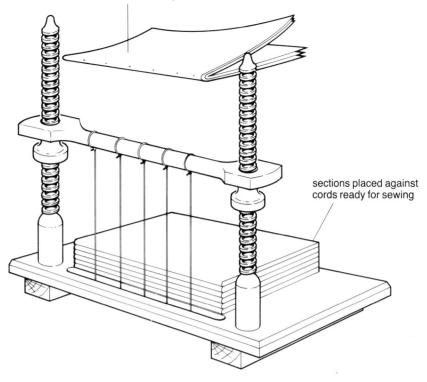

section marked up for cords

sections placed against cords ready for sewing

A binder's sewing frame, on which the sections of the book are sewn onto the cords. The cords can be seen as bands on the spines of most leather-bound books.

Hartmann Schopper, *Panoplia omnium artium*, 1543. Woodcut of binding.

Under the window a man is sewing the sections of the book onto cords in the sewing frame. In the foreground the binder is trimming the edges with the plough, the book held in a lying press. Another lying press in the bottom left of the picture holds a book ready for tooling. Various crude-looking tools hang on a wall, and the whole scene makes it difficult to believe that a fine binding, such as must often have been made in shops like this, will be the final product.

Good plain bindings were covered in pigskin, vellum or calf. More expensive bindings, from the sixteenth century onwards, were covered in goatskin, known as 'morocco' or 'turkey' according to its origin, and cheaper ones in leather from the skins of sheep. These two leathers are very different, because of the methods of tanning, although the skins themselves are quite similar. The imported morocco or turkey leather is close-grained, can be stained rich shades of red, blue, olive-green, brown or black, and takes a deep polish. Locally tanned sheep leather, on the other hand, is open-grained and porous-looking; it is soft to the touch and is usually a pale tan colour. To confuse the issue, in the late eighteenth century sheep was sometimes stained to imitate morocco and separating the sheep from the turkeys can be difficult.

Leather bindings were mostly done individually, to the order of the purchaser of the book or a few at a time for the individual retailer to sell over the counter. Some printers and publishers had always covered their books in temporary paper bindings, rather than issue them in unbound sheets; in the eighteenth century this practice became universal in Europe. The intention was that the customer would have his books bound in leather and discard the paper-covered binding, but inevitably, as the publishers' bindings were adequate for limited use, many readers did not wish to go to the trouble and expense of binding. Booksellers now describe books which survive in their publishers' bindings as in 'original boards', or 'original boards uncut', referring to the fact that the edges of

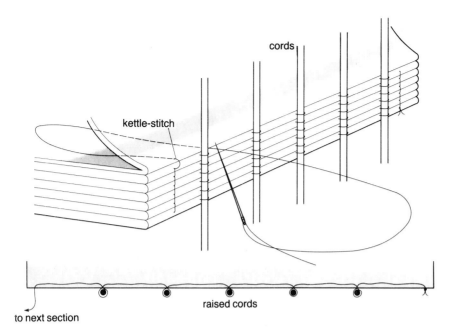

Two methods of sewing the sections of the book onto the cords in the sewing frame (a) on raised cords, which gives the spine the well-known ridged appearance; (b) on 'recessed' cords, which produces a flat spine.

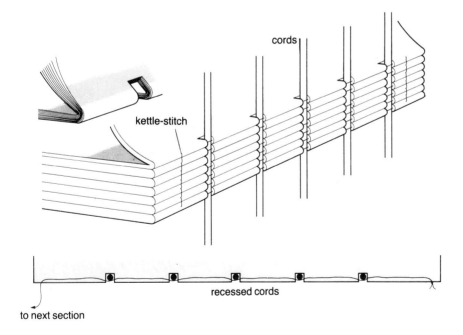

the pages were left untrimmed, and such copies are keenly sought after by some collectors. In the early nineteenth century publishers, beginning with William Pickering in 1820, started to cover the boards with cloth instead of paper so that the customer had a reasonably durable binding from the moment he bought it. Thus the appearance of the book changed dramatically, though not immediately its method of construction, and the modern hard-cover book was born.

The construction of a leather-bound book. The cords, onto which the sections are sewn, are firmly attached to the boards before the leather covering is applied. By this stage the headband would normally be attached.

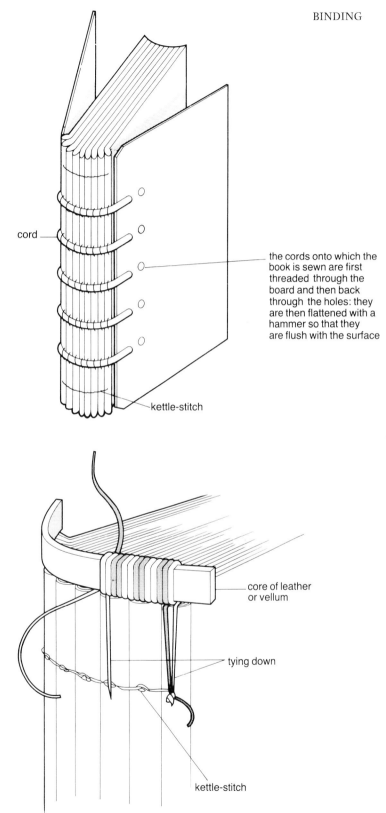

cord

the cords onto which the book is sewn are first threaded through the board and then back through the holes: they are then flattened with a hammer so that they are flush with the surface

kettle-stitch

core of leather or vellum

tying down

kettle-stitch

Sewing on a headband.

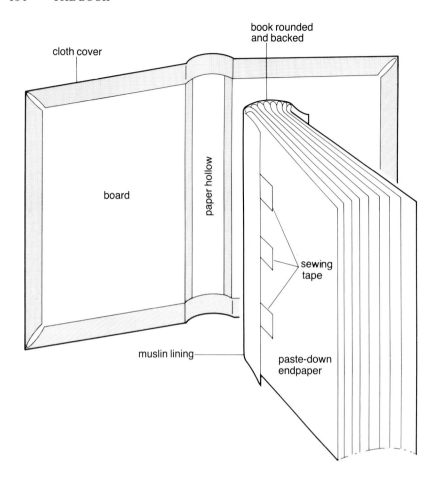

book rounded
and backed

cloth cover

board

paper hollow

sewing
tape

muslin lining

paste-down
endpaper

The construction of a cloth-bound or 'cased' book. Unlike the leather-bound book, the cloth-covered boards are manufactured separately and are only attached to the text block by pasting the tapes and the lining to the inside of the boards. Such bindings are therefore not as strong as leather bindings, in which the sewing cords are laced onto the boards.

At first cloth-covered bindings were constructed by hand in the same way as leather-covered bindings, as were the paper-covered bindings with which they co-existed for several decades, the sections sewn onto cords, or more often tapes, and the cords or tapes attached to the outside of the boards before the cloth covering was applied. Later, as the process became mechanized, the sections were sewn one to the next and not onto cords or tapes, which were replaced by a piece of gauze or mull glued across the back. The free edges of the mull were then glued to the insides of the boards of a prefabricated case. The mull can usually be seen showing through the pasted-down endpapers. Cloth-covered bindings are constructed with hollow spines, in contrast to earlier leather-covered bindings, in which the leather was glued directly to the back of the sections. Nineteenth-century leather bindings (rich bookbuyers liked to have their new books specially leather-bound as before, and a few still do) usually followed this hollow-backed style, which gave the book a more rigid spine which was easier to decorate.

The hand work of binding was only mechanized in the second half of the nineteenth century. First, powered guillotines were introduced to trim the edges, which had previously been left 'uncut'; however, throughout the nineteenth century books were often issued uncut and had to be 'opened' with a paper-knife, an essential tool for the Victorian novel reader. The two terms 'uncut' and 'unopened' are often confused and should perhaps be explained here. When the sheets of a book have been folded the edges have a rough appearance as the leaves never quite line up because of the paper taken up in the fold; this is true even of machine-made paper. A book in this state (that is, where the edges of the page have not been trimmed) is said to be 'uncut'. In books bound by hand the edges are trimmed with a kind of plane, called a plough; the unbound book is held tightly in a vice while this is done. When the edges have been trimmed all the pages separate. However, if the book has not been touched by the plough then certain leaves in each gathering will remain joined together by their top edges until opened with a paper-knife. A book whose joined leaves have not been slit in this way is said to be 'unopened'. Thus a book which is unopened is always uncut; but an uncut book may have been opened by a reader. After the introduction of guillotines for cutting paper accurately in quantity, there followed from the middle of the nineteenth century steam-powered machines for folding, sewing, rounding and backing, case-making, gathering, and, in 1903, casing-in.

Pamphlets are usually 'stab-sewn', that is the sewing-threads go through the leaves from front to back, half an inch or so into the inner margin, and back again and not through the fold. Even quite thick books of several sections were sometimes sent out from the printers like this, often sewn into a paper wrapper. Another special kind of sewing is found where single leaves, such as separately printed plates, have to be bound into books. Here there would be no natural fold to sew through and so the paper is sometimes left a little wide and folded at the inner edge, or it is 'guarded', that is, a narrow strip of folded paper is pasted along the inner edge to sew through; either method means that there is a disturbing 'stub' on the other side which looks as if it were the remains of a plate which has been removed. Alternatively single leaves can be 'overcast' or sewn through the inner edge. This is never very satisfactory, for if the sewing is too tight the book will not lie flat and it will be difficult to use; and if the sewing is loose, the thread will tear the edges of the paper as the book is opened. Libraries sometimes have overcasting machines, for 'restoring' books, which trim off the backs and overcast the whole volume: collectors will avoid such relics.

In modern paperback books the sheets are folded in the old way, though each sheet contains more pages, and then all the edges are trimmed off, making the book into a block of single leaves which are joined again by adhesive applied to the cut back. Interestingly, this technique was invented in about 1840, but it was found that the natural 'gutta-percha' or 'caoutchouc' adhesives decayed, leaving the book an untidy pile of separate sheets; 'perfect' binding, as it was optimistically called, was thus abandoned until the development of modern synthetic glues suggested to publishers that they might try it again. As every paperback reader knows, the leaves still fall out.

4. Care and Conservation

STORAGE

Old books do not require very special conditions or sophisticated storage or display cabinets, and are usually considered a pleasant addition to the decoration of any house. Space is sometimes a problem but bookshelves are simple to put up almost anywhere that you can find some free wall space. Security against theft is also less of a difficulty than with some precious objects, as many rare books are not obviously valuable and only the most sophisticated thief would know which books in a collection are of value. For this reason it is better to erase prices and keep cuttings from booksellers' catalogues separate from the books. Any fire extinguishers should be of the dry type: small fires usually only burn the backs off books, but water, either from flooding or when used to put out fires, is a major hazard as it will cause very unsightly staining. The bottom shelf of each bookcase should be a few inches off the floor if there is any danger of flooding. Otherwise, the rules for the physical storage of books are fairly obvious: don't pull books off the shelf by the head-band, don't let them lean over, as this strains the joints (folios are often better stored on their sides), keep them away from direct sunlight, and avoid extremes of temperature and humidity. The most crucial factor is the environment— both temperature and humidity—discussed below with reference to paper and bindings, and summarized at the end.

PAPER

Well-made paper is fortunately a very durable material, and in bound books, where it is protected against light and atmospheric pollutants, its conservation need not cause much anxiety if the books are kept in normal domestic conditions. The paper used by even the earliest printers has survived in beautiful condition for 500 years or more without any special conservation treatment and often still has a satisfyingly fresh feel and appearance, often described as 'crisp' in booksellers' catalogues. There are, however, two kinds of paper deterioration (mostly affecting nineteenth- and twentieth-century paper) which can be worrying to the collector. These are 'browning', an all-over discoloration, and 'foxing' or localized brown spots; the other problems described below result from misuse and can be avoided, if not remedied.

Browning

This is apparently caused by chemicals in the paper or in the size. It is occasionally noticed that a particular book is affected by browning in every copy, sometimes just in one particular signature, owing to the chemical make-up of a particular batch of paper. German paper of the seventeenth century, for instance, is often browned, presumably because a tradition of paper-making at that time left chemicals in the paper, later resulting in discoloration. The most common, and dangerous, agent in paper is acid, which promotes chemical decay, causing discoloration and making the paper brittle. This is a very serious problem with cheap twentieth-century wood-pulp paper and it is something that the private collector can do little about, since the only treatment—disbinding, washing and de-acidification of each leaf before rebinding—is a complicated and expensive process. Libraries can do it for a few of their more prized volumes, but the long-term future for the bulk of modern paperbacks and newspapers is causing librarians a lot of problems. A cool, dry atmosphere does retard or halt the chemical processes of browning and is really the only 'treatment' one can give, whilst making sure that any new paper introduced into the book is acid-free, as the acidity and browning can be transferred.

Foxing

This is the term used to describe the yellowish-brown, coffee- or rust-coloured irregular small stains which occasionally affect all books but which are especially troublesome in nineteenth-century books. Sadly, the paper used for printing colour plates seems particularly susceptible, and whereas some occasional foxing in the text of a book may be overlooked it can ruin a hand-coloured plate. The cause of most foxing is still not fully understood, but there do seem to be several, probably linked, factors. Mould is one cause, but is not invariably present. Chemical peculiarities, including high acidity, can be detected in foxed areas, but this could be either cause or effect. One type of foxing which is more clearly defined is caused by the rusting or oxidization of small particles of iron, copper or other metals present as impurities in the paper. Sometimes these can be detected in the centre of a stain, in which case they should be carefully removed to prevent the stain spreading further. Storage in a reasonably dry and cool environment should be enough to prevent or retard foxing, whether chemical or biological; libraries with conservation workshops sometimes also use fumigation and de-acidification. The benefit of removing existing foxing is, however, debatable. Professional paper conservationists can remove the stains either by washing the whole sheet or by localized application of bleaching agents, followed by washing and de-acidification, and resizing. Many claim that the results are perfect, but there is a risk that the delicate colours of hand-coloured plates will suffer and it is almost always possible to detect a difference in the feel and appearance of the paper. There are do-it-yourself reagents for removing foxing, but because of the danger of damaging a valuable article and the long-term risks associated with incomplete washing and de-acidification, it is best to leave these alone.

A particular problem sometimes found with illustrated books is the foxing of tissue guards. These were inserted when the book was bound to prevent the ink of the page of text facing a plate from offsetting onto the plate, and vice versa. For some reason the unsized tissue paper used is often more susceptible to foxing than the text and plate papers, and the foxing of the tissues can be transferred to the latter. The remedy is to remove all the tissues if there is the slightest trace of foxing in them and to replace them (although the ink is probably now dry enough not to offset) with new acid-free tissue.

Waterstaining

Books do seem to have a habit of getting wet from time to time and are surprisingly often affected by dampstaining. Perhaps it only appears to be so because other artefacts—paintings, porcelain, even furniture—do not always tell tales. Waterstaining usually takes the form of a light-brown or greyish stain behind a clearly defined and slightly darker tide mark. Waterstains can be washed out after the book has been disbound, but washed and resized paper is never quite the same and the result is not usually worth the expense, a washed book being only slightly, if at all, preferable to a waterstained one.

Soiling

Dust-soiling and dirty finger-marks can usually be partially or completely removed with a very soft eraser, or with fresh white bread used in the same way.

Torn and Damaged Paper

Extensive paper repairs, multiple tears on soft or brittle paper, piecing-in missing corners, tissue-lining and so on, are all jobs for the expert (bookbinders usually undertake paper repairs or have contacts with paper conservationists), but quite a lot of useful remedial work can be done at home. Clean tears are the thing to tackle first, and these should be mended as soon as possible or they may get worse each time the book is opened. Use paste (boiled flour and water is fine, or some proprietary mix or made-up paste), but not modern synthetic glue which may discolour; and any paper you introduce must be either old rag paper or new acid-free paper from an artist's supplier. Tears can often be repaired by carefully pasting the torn edges (not the surface of the paper), laying a piece of tissue paper on either side and closing the book with a piece of white blotting paper on each side of the invalid leaf. When the paste has had time to dry out, the tissues should be torn off, leaving behind a few fibres helping to hold the tear. This is not a very strong mend but it is quite adequate for normal use and it can be almost invisible on a fresh tear. If there is no text on the back of a page—for example a title-page or plate—a stronger repair can be made by pasting a piece of matching paper to the blank side; this is in fact the only way to mend the tears which almost always occur in folded plates. Tear the edges of the patch, rather than cutting them, to avoid a hard line. If you are unlucky enough to be faced with a page once mended with clear sticky tape, the tape now dry and detached leaving a nasty yellow stain, send it to your binder, who may be able to remove the stain and mend the leaf properly. Another simple operation which you can do yourself is the 'tipping in' of detached leaves or plates with a little paste along the extreme inner margin.

Facsimiles and Making Up

Even the most fastidious collector may for one reason or another wish to 'perfect' an incomplete copy of a book and this can be done either by adding the missing leaf or leaves from another (more imperfect) copy—provided it is of the same edition—or by inserting facsimile leaves. The best facsimiles are printed from photographs on old paper (old endpapers or other scraps of antique paper are always carefully saved by binders who sometimes do this sort of work). The results can be very convincing. The questions of ethics and taste are discussed earlier (see pp.43–8); but the detection of such facsimiles is usually easy for the experienced eye, as it is almost impossible to match the paper exactly. Most modern photocopiers will print well on ordinary paper and surprisingly good facsimiles can be made by photocopying onto old paper, or sympathetic modern paper, and this is a good way to have a copy of the original: it will fool no one, but neither will it look out of place. Uncoloured plates can be copied in this way, but there is no adequate way of reproducing colour plates and it is probably best to obtain a colour photograph of the missing print for reference and keep it separate from the book.

BINDINGS

Most repair and conservation work on books involves the bindings, sensitive as they are to handling, to fluctuations in temperature and humidity, and to atmospheric pollutants. Leather bindings can withstand a lot of use if properly looked after; cloth bindings can be safely left alone but deteriorate quickly with use; and paper-covered boards or paper wrappers are the most fragile of all.

Leather Bindings

The vulnerable parts of a leather-bound book are the head and foot of the spine, which are damaged by careless handling in taking the book off the shelf and putting it back, and the joints and corners. The first part of the joint to go is usually the leather forming the outer joint: with continued heavy use the thongs or cords to which the sections of the book are sewn and which attach the boards to the book will crack or wear through, and as the paper inner hinges have no strength and are probably already split, the boards will come off.

If the boards are detached, you will probably want to have the book repaired, but it is important always to consider what the conservationists call the 'integrity' (although it is now in three pieces) of the original binding. Some collectors may prefer not to interfere with the original binding in any way, and simply tie a piece of soft tape round the book (not a rubber band, which soon perishes and can scuff the leather when removed). This is an unsightly expedient. An alternative is to have a case made for it; this is costly, but no more so than having the binding repaired. If the binding is to be repaired it is obviously important that as much as possible of the original should be preserved. Usually it is possible to re-back a book whose boards have become detached: this means that the boards are re-attached and a new leather spine worked over the back and under the old leather which covers the sides; this should be pared down to make a smooth join. You should ask your binder to lay down the old spine on the new leather if it can be saved. This is often the cheaper option, as it means that there is no lettering or other tooling to do, but it may be more expensive if the old spine is fragile and difficult to remove in one piece; it may then be necessary to re-gild the parts which have been renewed. It is best to discuss any repair work with the binder first as his view and yours as to what is worth saving may differ: always insist on re-using the old endpapers, which some binders have a habit of discarding. A simple re-backing job on an octavo, where the old spine comes away easily and can be laid down again, might cost £15 or £20; if the old spine is difficult to save and the binder does some geniune gold tooling (using individual tools and gold leaf, not foil) it might be £25 to £30 or more.

There is always the question of restoration or conservation in binding repairs. Booksellers and collectors generally prefer restoration and are happy to tool new leather in imitation of the original, and even stain and batter it for greater authenticity; libraries often follow this practice too. However, some librarians take the view, more common in other areas of museum conservation work, that any new work should be left plain and honest. If the original binding is so far gone that nothing can sensibly be saved, both private and institutional collectors prefer a new binding which is in keeping with the period and national origin of the book in terms of materials and style, is simply decorated and does not attempt to reproduce an old binding. Booksellers, presumably with no intention of misleading their customers, traditionally describe such bindings as 'antique', as in 'calf antique', genuinely old bindings being described as 'contemporary', or of a specified date or period.

Paper and Cloth Bindings

Paper and cloth-covered bindings can be re-backed and otherwise repaired in much the same way as leather bindings. However, it is worth re-emphasizing the point, made elsewhere in this book, that paper-covered boards or a cloth binding are an integral part of the book as originally issued and any repair detracts from its bibliographical completeness in a way that it does not for leather-bound books. Given the weakness of paper- and cloth-bound books, individual cases are very worth while. Cloth- or leather-covered clam-shell cases are obviously the best, but they are expensive and not very satisfying to have on the shelf. An excellent alternative is to make your own cardboard slip-cases, which leave the spines exposed. Similarly you can make simple card folding cases for pamphlets, which are otherwise impossible to shelve safely.

Cleaning and Oiling Leather Bindings

Leather bindings should not be washed, even with a mild soap such as saddle soap, as there is a danger of washing out the salts present in traditionally tanned, or specially prepared modern, leathers. These salts provide protection against atmospheric pollutants, especially sulphur dioxide; without this protection, acids accumulate in the leather, which then quickly decays and becomes crumbly. A careful application of the British Museum formula leather dressing is all that is necessary to clean neglected books and anyone who has used it on an old book will know how much grime comes off on the cotton wool. Apart from cleaning the bindings, the dressing serves the more important function of replenishing the oils in the leather which keep it supple and help prevent cracked joints. Before the advent of central heating, which dries out the leather of bindings, enough grease was probably added from the hands each time a book was used. When applying the dressing, be sure to avoid getting it on the edges of the book as these would absorb the grease: manuals instruct you to wrap the text block in brown paper before you begin and to hold the book shut while applying the dressing. The volumes should be left standing overnight, not touching each other, and should be polished with a soft cloth the next day. Other leather dressings and hide foods should be used with caution, as some appear to damage the gold tooling.

Vellum Bindings

These can be washed with a slightly damp sponge, dried quickly in a good draught and polished with a very little leather dressing.

Cleaning Cloth Bindings

A special cloth restorer is manufactured for cloth bindings: this can improve the appearance of discoloured cloth by redistributing the dye over the stained or faded area and at the same time re-dressing the cloth. It will also brighten up dull cloth which has not been misused but it must be used with caution as it can take off gilding, stain paper labels and change the colour and texture of the cloth and it does nothing actually to preserve the binding.

ENVIRONMENT

The temperature at which books are stored is not as critical as the humidity; but the humidity is itself affected by the temperature. If the book is too damp—an unlikely situation in most modern homes—mildew or other moulds, whose spores are always present, can thrive on paper and bindings. If it is too dry the paper may become brittle, and the boards may warp as the leather or other covering shrinks more than the paper lining, probably splitting the joints at top and bottom (which are already weakened if the leather has dried out). Worst of all are fluctuating conditions, pulling the binding this way and that as its many components swell and contract at different rates.

The important thing to remember about humidity is that the air will hold more moisture the warmer it is, and we measure 'percentage relative humidity', that is the percentage saturation at the prevailing temperature. As the temperature rises, the same amount of moisture represents a lower and lower relative humidity, or conversely the same relative humidity means more moisture in the air at higher temperatures. A book, or any other object, will dry out if the surrounding air is less saturated with water than the fibres of the leather, paper, etc., and this will always happen if the temperature is raised without raising the absolute humidity. Books should be kept at a relative humidity of between 40 and 50 per cent and to maintain this it may therefore be necessary artificially to humidify the atmosphere as the temperature is raised. A hygrometer to measure the humidity should be purchased if you are concerned about the atmosphere surrounding your books.

The environment for books preferred by library conservators is a temperature of 60° Fahrenheit or less, and a relative humidity of 40 to 50 per cent. Most people find this uncomfortably cold and 60° to 70° is probably a better compromise between books and their owners. Above 70° you should be prepared for foxing and browning to spread; below 50° the necessity to lower the absolute humidity becomes acute, as the relative humidity will rise sharply if not artificially lowered, and the books will become damp and mildewed.

Glossary

Special terms and jargon words differ widely in the book trade and among book collectors. Some of these words are not commonly used today, but may still be found in old reference books and catalogues. More complete lists will be found in John Carter's *ABC for Book Collectors* (5th edition, London and New York, 1972), an idiosyncratic guide to terminology in the antiquarian book trade; and in Jean Peters, *The Bookman's Glossary* (6th edition, London and New York, 1983), which deals with all aspects of the book, both contemporary and antiquarian. For reading book catalogues in other languages, Menno Hertzberger's *Dictionary for the Antiquarian Book Trade* (Paris, 1956) is useful, though it is now out of print and difficult to obtain.

American incunabula: books printed in the seventeenth century (i.e. before 1701) in what is now the United States of America. See also *incunabula*.

Americana: in the developed sense, printed and manuscript material dealing with the history of the United States of America—its discovery, geography and literature. More broadly, any material relating to the history of the continent, including Canada, South America and the West Indies. *USiana* is the unlikeable term occasionally employed for books relating solely to the United States.

Antique: of bindings, modern imitations of old styles. Thus 'calf antique' or 'antique-style morocco' means that the binding is not original but a modern reproduction.

Aquatint: a process in copperplate etching which produces continuous tone (rather than lines). Often used as a basis for hand-coloured plates in imitation of watercolours.

Armorial binding: any binding with the heraldic arms of the original (or sometimes a later) owner stamped, usually in gilt, on the covers.

Association copy: strictly, a copy of a book whose early ownership is associated with the author. Occasionally this is broadened to include copies owned by friends, interesting contemporaries or notable later students of the author.

Auction: a selling occasion at which books (or, indeed, other objects) are offered for sale to the highest bidder. In common speech in Britain an auction is often called a *sale*, but the proper term is usually preferred in America to avoid confusion with cut-price offers by retailers.

Autograph: anything (not just a signature) written by its author. 'Autograph letter signed' has a different meaning from 'letter signed': the latter would be in the hand of an amanuensis or typed by a secretary, but signed by its author, and the former both written and signed by the author.

Bibliography: (a) the history and scientific description of printed books. (b) A list of books selected and ordered according to a scientific method—alphabetical, chronological, or other. A bibliography of a particular author should list and describe all the early editions of his or her works, and perhaps some related material.

Binding: the boards, thread, endpapers and covering (usually leather or cloth) which protect the leaves of a book; the process of giving the book this covering.

Blank: an unprinted leaf which forms part of the original book.

Blind-tooled: (of a binding) decorated by impressing the tools onto the surface without the use of colour or gold.

Block book: a book printed from wooden blocks in which each page, both words and pictures, is carved from a single piece of wood and cannot be rearranged for subsequent use; a technique briefly employed in the mid-fifteenth century.

Board, boards: the sides of a binding decorated with pasteboard or wood and covered or decorated with paper, leather or cloth.

Broadside: a single sheet printed on one side and issued by itself, used for advertisements, ballads, propaganda, etc.

Burin: the engraver's instrument for gouging lines on the copper or steel plate.

Calf: tanned calfskin used for binding.

Called for: booksellers' jargon meaning 'required by the relevant authority': thus, 'only 23 plates, as called for by Upcott' would indicate that Upcott thinks that the book was intended to have only 23 plates when issued, although other bibliographers may differ.

Cancel: if a mistake is made in printing which might be corrected by the deletion of a single leaf from the finished quire, another leaf is sometimes printed and stuck on a stub from which the original has been cut away. The leaf excised is said to be *cancelled* (properly it is the 'cancellandum') and the substitute is a *cancel* (properly the 'cancellans').

Case, cased: (a) prefabricated binding of cloth-bound books. (b)

Various types of additional cases for the protection of fragile books. The most frequently found is the *slipcase*; another is the *solander* case. (c) The cases used by printers. These were like trays, and held founts of type in their compartments. The upper tray held the capitals, the lower the small letters; thus 'upper case' and 'lower case' letters mean capital and small letters to printers.

Chain lines: the vertical lines seen in a sheet of handmade paper, usually about 2 cm (1 in.) apart, which hold the wires in place in the original paper mould.

Character: a single letter; sometimes, a single piece of type (although single types may contain more than one letter of the alphabet—see *ligature*).

Chase: the steel frame in which metal type is locked so that it can be laid on the press for printing.

Chromolithography: printing in colours by the process of *lithography*.

Cloth, original cloth: cloth-bound books (books 'in cloth') are what we now call 'hardback books'. Most books were issued by their publishers in cloth from the fourth decade of the nineteenth century (original cloth); books which have been re-bound are described as being in 'binder's cloth', or worse still in 'library cloth'. The cloth used may be linen (buckram), cotton or silk.

Codex, codices: the standard book format, in which folded flat sheets are stitched along one edge to bind the sheets together.

Collate: (a) to gather the sheets of an unbound book in sequence for binding. (b) To check the physical make-up of a book to verify its completeness: this may involve plates and elements of the binding (such as the dust-jacket) as well as leaves.

Colophon: information about the place and date of printing given by the printer at the end of the text if there is no title page.

Commission: a bookseller who buys at auction (or privately) on behalf of his customer is said to be buying 'on commission'. The charge for this service is usually 10 per cent.

Compose: to put single letters of type together for printing. A 'compositor' in the hand press period held a 'composing stick' in which he assembled the type from his case before transferring it to the *galley*.

Copperplate: a flat plate of copper was used for printing fine images (see pp. 126–7); the picture thus produced was called a copperplate engraving, or simply *plate*.

Corrigenda: similar to *errata*, for which extra slips or pages are sometimes printed, but meaning corrections to the text by the author rather than errors by the printer made good.

Cover: the board or side of a bookbinding.

Deckle: the feathery edge to hand-made paper caused by seepage between the frame on which the paper is made and the rim or deckle which is placed round the frame to prevent the pulp spilling over the side.

Dentelle: the decorated edge of the leather which the binder brings over the board from the outside of the binding. Sometimes called the 'turn-in'.

Duodecimo: a book with quires of twelve leaves. Abbreviated to 12mo.

Dust-jacket: the paper cover issued with books from the mid-nineteenth century onwards, at first to protect the binding but later as a surface for advertising the book or for decoration.

Edition: in the hand press period, a fresh setting in type of a book. Modern publishers often use the word to indicate a new *issue* or *impression* of a book.

Endpapers, endleaves: plain leaves inserted by the binder between the boards and the text of the book. The 'pastedown' is the endpaper stuck down onto the board, the 'free endpaper' is part of the same sheet folded back and cut to match the edges of the leaves.

Engraving: an illustration printed from an engraved copper or steel plate.

Errata: errors in the printing of a book which are recognized too late for corrections to be made in the text. A separate slip or an extra leaf may be printed to bring the faults to the reader's attention. See also *corrigenda*.

Etching: an illustration printed from an etched metal plate, usually copper (see p. 127).

Extra-illustrated: copies of books in which additional illustrations, manuscripts and other material has been added. This practice was popular in the nineteenth and early twentieth centuries.

Facsimile: an exact reproduction, by photography or by typographic or manuscript imitation, of an original leaf or book.

Fetch: booksellers' jargon for 'sell for', when a lot is sold at auction.

Folio: a single leaf, especially a leaf of a book printed with two leaves to each *quire* (a 'folio' book—see p. 122). Abbreviations: f. (when a single leaf), 2o. or fo. (when meaning a book printed in folio).

Fore-edge painting: a painting executed on the fore-edges of a book held open obliquely. The edges of the closed book are then gilded so that the painting only appears when the book is fanned open again.

Format: a bibliographical term for the way the sheet is folded to make the sections of a book—this also gives a rough idea of its size and shape (folio, quarto, octavo, etc.)

Forme: a group of pages of printer's type in the *chase* ready for printing. (See illustration on p. 116.)

Fount: a set of types, created to one design and complete with all necessary ligatures, capitals, figures, etc. Pronounced 'font'.

Foxing: irregular brown spots or stains in paper caused by chemical or metallic impurities in the original stock, often aggravated by poor storage.

Frisket: a light wooden or metal frame which folds down over the *tympan*, holding the paper in place and keeping it from contact with the *chase* or *furniture*. The frisket is covered with paper or parchment cut out to allow only the type to print.

Furniture: wooden or metal blocks to pack out the type in the chase.

Galley: a metal tray on which the composed lines of type are placed before making up into pages; hence 'galley proofs' are proofs of the text before it is divided into pages.

Gathering: see *quire*.

Guard, guarded: the strip of paper pasted to the edge of an engraved plate or other leaf printed singly. Without being thus 'guarded' such leaves cannot be sewn securely into the book.

Halftone: an illustration printed from an image which has been broken up into a regular pattern of dots. May be printed by letterpress or lithography.

Half calf, half morocco, half vellum: half bindings, a cheaper style of binding common from the beginning of the nineteenth century, used ordinary binding leathers or vellum but only in the places of most wear—on the spine and at the corners—the rest of the boards being covered with marbled or plain paper, or cloth.

Hand: the handwriting of a person. 'Lincoln's hand was clean' refers not to the President's personal hygiene but to the characteristics of his penmanship.

Headband: the cotton or silk whipped cord which strengthens the top of the spine of a book. In leather-bound books the headband is sewn to the tops of the sections; in cased books it is glued to the back of the sections. Many modern cased books do without headbands.

Hinge: the inside join between the board and the back of the book. See *joint*.

Holograph: a document wholly in the *hand* of its author.

Hot metal: casting type from molten metal at the moment of composition: Monotype and Linotype are the two most common hot metal processes.

House sale: an auction held on the premises of the house whose contents are being sold. Books, which need precise cataloguing, are often excluded from house sales if the library is valuable, as they can be better sold on the auctioneer's own ground.

Imperfect: see *perfect*.

Imposition: the plan for arranging the pages so that when the book is finished the margins are uniform and the pages run consecutively.

Impression: (a) in modern printing, the issue of a new printing from the old setting of type, often used synonymously with *edition*. (b) A single print from type or a plate, as in 'fine impression'.

Imprint: the statement of place, publisher/printer and date found in most books at the foot of the title page. Where the printer is not the publisher, he may add his own 'imprint' on the back of the title page or after the end of the text. This is common from the late eighteenth century on.

Incunabula: books printed with movable type before 1501. From the Latin meaning 'things from the cradle': the singular is technically 'incunabulum' but most people say 'incunable'.

Inscription: anything written by hand in a book, but usually indicating a message presenting the book or recording owner-ship. Usefully avoids the possibly confusing use of the word *signature*.

Issue: bibliographical term which is precisely defined but often difficult to use with equal precision. An issue is a bibliographi-cally distinct group of books which form part of an *edition*. Copies of one issue must differ from those of another in some typograph-ical way and yet be composed largely of sheets printed from the same setting of type. Common 'second issues' are those in which one or more leaves have been *cancelled*, or where a book sold badly and was 'reissued' with a new title page, masquerading as a new *edition*.

Joint: the outside join between the board and the back of the book.

Laid paper: paper showing a pattern of wide and narrow spaced lines when held up to the light. It can be hand-made or machine made.

Large paper copy: one of a small number of de luxe copies of an edition printed on larger paper than the ordinary copies. Large paper copies generally have very wide margins, but this is no guarantee that your copy is on large paper—you may find that all copies are like that.

Leaf: commonly, but wrongly, called a *page*. One leaf = two pages.

Letterpress: printing from raised type.

Ligature: two letters cut together by the punchcutter, e.g. f and l, or f and f. Commoner in early printing, where punchcutters strove to reproduce manuscript forms.

Limp vellum: a binding style common in Europe in the sixteenth and seventeenth centuries in which the book cover is made from a sheet of vellum without any stiffening.

Line block: printing block for *letterpress* printing, usually made photographically from a line drawing. Used to reproduce printed pages in making facsimiles.

Lithograph: literally, 'drawing on stone', but used for any print from a flat surface (see pp. 127–30).

Making-up, made-up: the now frowned-on practice of 'perfecting' an incomplete copy of a book by supplying missing leaves from another, presumably worse, copy.

Matrix: the small block of copper stamped with a single letter which fits into the typefounder's mould in which the types are cast.

Mezzotint: a technique of copperplate engraving in which the whole surface of the plate is roughened to print solid black and the design is made by smoothing it down again to produce graded tones.

Morocco: tanned goatskin used for binding, originally produced in North Africa.

Mottled: of calf skin or sheepskin using in bindings, the decorative effect produced by dabbing or sprinkling the leather with dilute acid. Fine mottling is often described as 'sprinkled'; very regular dabs as 'cat's paw calf'.

Movable type: printing type as invented by Gutenberg in the fifteenth century, in which each letter is on a separate piece of metal.

Not subject to return: a lot in an auction catalogue sold *with all faults*, for which the house 'conditions of sale' relating to the cancellation of the sale do not apply. In many provincial and low-value auctions all lots are sold 'not subject to return'.

Octavo: bibliographical term for the most common book *format* in which there are eight leaves in each quire.

Offset: the unsightly transference of ink from a page of text or a plate onto the facing page.

Original: booksellers' jargon meaning 'as published', e.g. 'original cloth'.

Owner's mark: a characteristic way of recording ownership, e.g. a collector may have always initialled p. 17 in his books.

Page: one side of a *leaf*.

Parchment: animal skin prepared for writing, printing or binding—in the latter cases usually called *vellum*.

Part: a single issue of a book published in separate instalments.

Pasteboard: stiff laminated cardboard used for the sides of books—usually covered with leather, cloth or paper.

Pastedown: see *endpaper.*

Perfect: complete as originally published, with the full complement of leaves and plates.

Periodical: serial publication of undefined duration, i.e. a newspaper but not a book published in *parts.*

Photogravure: a method of reproducing artwork or photographs from a photographically produced *intaglio* plate.

Photolithography: a method of reproducing artwork or photographs from a photographically produced *lithographic* plate.

Plate: a single leaf on which an illustration is printed (by any process). An engraved plate was almost always printed separately from the text of the book.

Platen: the flat (sometimes cylindrical) surface in the printing press which presses the paper onto the type.

Plough: the bookbinder's plane used to trim the edges of the bound book.

Points: (a) the pins which hold the paper in place in the printing press to ensure accurate *registration.* (b) The bibliographical features which distinguish one *issue* from another.

Preliminaries: all the leaves of a book which precede the main text, e.g. the title-page, table of contents, preface. Abbreviated to 'prelims'.

Presentation copy: a copy of a book which has been given by someone connected with it, usually the author, to another person—preferably important.

Press: (a) machine for printing by whatever process. (b) A firm engaged in printing.

Proof: a trial impression of text or illustration. Proofs of copper plates, 'proof plates', are highly valued because copper plates wear during the print run and early impressions will be clearer and sharper.

Quarter calf, quarter morocco: a binding style in which only the spine of the book is covered in leather, the sides being covered with paper or cloth—see *half calf,* etc.

Quarto: bibliographical term for a book with four leaves in each quire.

Quire: the group of leaves which are folded together before the book is bound. Sometimes called *section, gathering* or *signature.*

Rag paper: paper made from a pulp of mashed rags.

Re-backed: having the joints of the binding repaired and the spine recovered.

Registration: the accurate alignment of text on each side of the leaf, or of the colours in colour illustration.

Rooms: in Britain, booksellers' jargon for auction houses.

Rounding and backing: the process in bookbinding by which the spine of the book is given its characteristic curved shape.

Runner: in Britain, booksellers' jargon for a trader who does not own any stock but who acts as a middleman between one dealer and another.

Running title (running head): the title of the book (or chapter) printed at the top of each page.

Resized: if old paper has been washed it is soft and porous until it has been 'resized'. See *sized.*

Roan: a cheap binding leather made from sheepskin.

Russia: a binding leather tanned in a particular way and impregnated with birch-bark oil. Common in Britain in the late eighteenth and early nineteenth centuries.

Sale: booksellers' jargon for *auction* (especially in Britain).

Signature: the letter and/or number at the foot of the first leaf of a quire, by which the printer identifies the quire. Hence the quire itself is sometimes called a 'signature'.

Size: the composition of gelatin, starch, etc. with which paper is treated to reduce its porosity. Blotting paper is simply unsized paper.

Slipcase: an open-ended box to protect a book.

Solander case: a closed box for a book made in two parts which fit into one another.

Spine: the back of the book, formed by the inner folds of the leaves and their covering.

Sprung: used to describe the condition of a book in which the spine has been weakened or cracked and individual gatherings are loose or the whole book is floppy.

Stab-sewn: of pamphlets which are sewn from front to back through the inner margin, rather than through the fold.

State: applied to text and illustrations, a distinct variety of impression identified in more than one copy, e.g. 'first state of the title with the misprint *London* uncorrected'.

Stereotype: a cast of the original setting of type from which a new impression of a book can be printed.

Stipple engraving: technique in copperplate engraving in which tone is built up by making tiny nicks in the plate which print as dots.

Tipped in: single plates or other leaves fastened into a book by being pasted along their inner edge.

Title, title page: the page, but usually taken to mean the whole leaf, on which the author's name, the title of the book and the publisher's or printer's imprint and the date of the edition are printed. In early books this information is usually supplied in the *colophon.*

Tool: in binding, the engraved punches which are used to impress the leather with each individual element of a design.

Tooling: the impressed decoration on a binding, often gilt.

Tree calf: of a binding in which the calf leather has been treated by running dilute acid over it to produce a grained effect, sometimes looking like the grain of fine wood.

Turkey: tanned goatskin (once imported from Turkey) used in binding—similar to if not indistinguishable from *morocco,* the modern term.

Turn-in: see *dentelle.*

Tympan: part of the hand printing press on which the paper is fixed and which then folds down onto the type.

Typeface: the design of the letters of a fount of type.

Typography: (a) printing from movable types. (b) More commonly, the aesthetics and craft of arranging the words and other matter (e.g. ornaments) on the printed page.

Uncut: used of a book in which the edges of the leaves have not been cut by a *plough*. To be distinguished from *unopened*.

Unopened: used of a book in which certain leaves are still joined together along their upper or outer edges.

USiana: see *Americana*.

Vellum: the skin of calves prepared for writing, printing or bookbinding. Books printed on vellum are always more expensive and luxurious than those on paper.

Vellum boards: binding style in which vellum is used as a covering over stiff pasteboard.

View, viewing days: bookseller's jargon for the public exhibition before an auction during which dealers and the public can examine the books.

Volume: the distinct physical object. One book may comprise several volumes.

w.a.f.: see *with all faults*.

Watermark: the papermaker's trademark made by a wire design fixed to the mould, seen when the paper is held up to the light.

Wire lines: the closely spaced lines in *laid paper*.

With all faults: auctioneers' jargon for a book sold *not subject to return*. (Often abbreviated to w.a.f.)

Woodcut: an illustration printed from a woodblock. In modern usage confined to blocks cut on the plank grain of fruit wood to distinguish them from *wood-engravings*.

Wood-engraving: an illustration printed from a block made by engraving on the end grain of a block of box wood.

Wove paper: paper which has no *chain lines* and *wire lines*, usually made on a woven mesh of wires.

Wrapper: a paper cover sewn or glued onto a book or pamphlet.

Xylography: pedantic word for printing from wood.

Yapp edges: the turn-in on the fore-edge of some vellum bindings.

Useful Addresses

AUCTION HOUSES

United Kingdom and Ireland

BLOOMSBURY BOOK AUCTIONS, 3 and 4 Hardwick Street, London
EC1R 4RY. Telephone: (01) 833 2636
BONHAM'S, Montpelier Street, London SW7 1HH.
Telephone: (01) 584 9161
CHRISTIE'S, 8 King Street, St James's, London SW1Y 6QT.
Telephone: (01) 839 9060
CHRISTIE'S SOUTH KENSINGTON, 85 Old Brompton Road, London
SW7 3JS. Telephone: (01) 581 7611
CHRISTIE'S AND EDMISTON'S, 164–6 Bath Street, Glasgow,
Scotland G2 4TG. Telephone: (041) 332 8134
LAWRENCE OF CREWKERNE, South Street, Crewkerne, Somerset
TA18 8AB. Telephone: (0460) 73041
GEORGE MEALY & SONS, Castlecomer, Co. Kilkenny, Ireland.
Telephone: (056) 41229
PHILLIPS, 7 Blenheim Street, New Bond Street, London W1Y 0AS.
Telephone: (01) 629 6602. Sales are also held at the firm's
offices in Edinburgh, Leeds and Oxford.
SOTHEBY'S, 34–5 New Bond Street, London W1A 2AA.
Telephone: (01) 493 8080
SOTHEBY'S PULBOROUGH, Pulborough, West Sussex RH20 1AJ.
Telephone: (07982) 3831
TAVINER'S, Prewett Street, Redcliffe, Bristol BS1 6PB.
Telephone: (0272) 25996

North America

CALIFORNIA BOOK AUCTION GALLERIES, 358 Golden Gate Avenue,
San Francisco, Ca. 94102
CHRISTIE'S INTERNATIONAL, 502 Park Avenue, New York,
NY 10022. Telephone: (212) 546 1000
SAMUEL T. FREEMAN & CO., 1808 Chestnut Street, Philadelphia,
Pa. 19103
PHILLIPS, 406 East 79th Street, New York, NY 10021.
Telephone: (212) 570 4830
SOTHEBY'S, 1334 York Avenue (at 72nd Street), New York,
NY 10021. Telephone: (212) 606 7000
SWANN GALLERIES, 104 East 25th Street, New York, NY 10010.
Telephone: (212) 254 4710

Continental Europe

CHRISTIE'S AMSTERDAM, Cornelis Schuytstraat 57, 1071 JG
Amsterdam, Netherlands

CHRISTIE'S ROME, 114 Piazza Navona, 00186 Roma, Italy
HARTUNG & KARL, Karolinenplatz 5a, D–8000 München 2, West
Germany
HAUSWEDELL & NOLTE, D–2000 Hamburg 13, Pöseldorfer Weg 1,
West Germany
HOTEL DROUOT, 9 Rue Drouot, 75009 Paris, France
DR HELMUT TENNER, Sofientstrasse 5, D–6900 Heidelberg 1, West
Germany
REISS & AUVERMANN, Zum Talblick 2, 6246 Glashütten im
Taunus 1, West Germany
SOTHEBY'S ITALIA, Palazzo Capponi, Via Gino Capponi 26,
Firenze, Italy
SOTHEBY'S MONACO, Sporting d'Hiver, Place du Casino, Monte
Carlo, MC 98000, Monaco
J. A. STARGARDT, Rädestrasse 10, D–3550 Marburg, West
Germany. Autographs and manuscripts only.
VAN GENDT, 96–8 Keizersgracht, 1015 CV Amsterdam,
Netherlands

Australasia and South Africa

CHRISTIE'S AUSTRALIA, 298 New South Head Road, Double Bay,
Sydney 2028, New South Wales, Australia
KENNETH HINCE, 140 Greville Street, Prahran, Victoria 3181,
Australia
SOTHEBY'S SOUTH AFRICA, PO Box 31010, Braamfontein 2017,
Johannesburg, Transvaal, South Africa
VOLKS RARE BOOK AUCTIONS, 222–4 Schubart Street, Pretoria,
Transvaal, South Africa

DEALERS

There are thousands of dealers throughout the English-speaking
world: here we list only a small selection which incorporates
most of the principal names. Regularly-issued guides published
by the Sheppard Press (Russell Chambers, Covent Garden,
London WC2E 8AX) give details of specialized antiquarian
dealers in Britain, North America and Europe, divided by area.
Many dealers now operate from their homes, and appointments
should therefore be made before visiting those designated
'Private premises'.

United Kingdom and Ireland

GEORGE BAYNTUN LTD., Manvers Street, Bath. Telephone:
(0225) 66000. Fine modern bindings, general.
BLACKWELL'S RARE BOOKS, Fyfield Manor, Fyfield, Abingdon,
Oxfordshire OX13 5LR. Telephone: (0865) 390692. English

literature, travel, modern first editions, bibliography.

CLAUDE COX, College Gateway Bookshop, 3 and 5 Silent Street, Ipswich IP1 1TF. Telephone: (0473) 54776. General, fine printing.

H. M. FLETCHER LTD., 27 Cecil Court, Charing Cross Road, London WC2N 4EZ. Telephone: (01) 836 2865. Secondhand and antiquarian.

GEORGE'S, 52 Park Street, Bristol BS1 5JN. Telephone: (0272) 276602. English literature, private press books, travel.

E. P. GOLDSCHMIDT & CO., 64 Drayton Gardens, London SW10 9SB. Telephone: (01) 373 2266. Early, illustrated and scientific books. Private premises.

HOWES BOOKSHOP, Trinity Hall, Braybrooke Terrace, Hastings, East Sussex TN34 1HQ. Telephone: (0424) 423437. Fine scholarly editions of literature, bibliography and theology.

JOHN GRANT, 13C and 15A Dundas Street, Edinburgh EH3 6QG. Telephone: (031) 556 9698. Scottish books, general.

E. JOSEPH LTD., 1 Vere Street, London W1M 9HQ. Telephone: (01) 493 8353. Modern illustrated and private press books, standard sets in fine bindings.

PATRICK KING, 36 Calverton Road, Stony Stratford, Buckinghamshire MK11 1HL. Telephone: (0908) 564546. Fine bindings and printing.

E. M. LAWSON & CO., Kingsholm, East Hagbourne, Oxfordshire. Telephone: (0235) 812033. Travel, early English literature, economics. Private premises.

MAGGS BROS. LTD., 50 Berkeley Square, London W1. Telephone: (01) 493 7160. Rare books and manuscripts of all periods.

MARLBOROUGH RARE BOOKS LTD., 35 Old Bond Street, London W1X 4PT. Telephone: (01) 493 6993. Illustrated books, architecture, bibliography and typography.

PICKERING & CHATTO LTD., 17 Pall Mall, London SW1Y 5NB. Telephone: (01) 930 2515. English literature, science and medicine, economics and history of ideas.

BERNARD QUARITCH LTD., 5–8 Lower John Street, Golden Square, London W1R 4AU. Telephone: (01) 734 2983. Rare books and manuscripts of all periods.

BERTRAM ROTA LTD., 30 and 31 Long Acre, London WC2E 9LT. Telephone: (01) 836 0723. Modern first editions, private press books, literature.

ROBERT D. STEEDMAN, 9 Grey Street, Newcastle upon Tyne NE1 6EE. Telephone: (0632) 326561. Travel and illustrated, English literature, standard sets.

ALAN G. THOMAS, c/o National Westminster Bank, 300 King's Road, Chelsea, London SW3. Telephone: (01) 352 5130. Incunabula, theology and bibles, English literature. Private premises.

ROBIN WATERFIELD LTD., 36 Park End Street, Oxford OX1 1HJ. Telephone: (0865) 721809. English literature, modern first editions, general.

WHELDON & WESLEY LTD., Lytton Lodge, Codicote, Hitchin, Hertfordshire SG4 8TE. Telephone: (0438) 820370. Natural history books. Private premises.

North America

JOHN F. FLEMING, 322 East 57th Street, New York, NY 10022. Telephone: (212) 755 3242. English literature. Private premises.

GOODSPEED'S BOOK SHOP, 7 Beacon Street, Boston, Ma. 02108. Telephone: (617) 523 5970. Americana, autographs, first editions.

HAMILL & BARKER, 400 North Michigan Avenue, Chicago, Il. 60611. Telephone: (312) 644 5933. First editions, illustrated books, incunabula.

HERITAGE BOOKSHOP, 847 North La Cienega Boulevard, Los Angeles, Ca. 90069. Telephone: (213) 659 3674. Modern literature, private press, general.

LATHROP C. HARPER, INC., 300 Madison Avenue, New York, NY 10017. Telephone: (212) 490 3412. Early literature, incunabula, science, manuscripts.

JONATHAN A. HILL, 470 West End Avenue, New York, NY 10024. Telephone: (212) 496 7856. Science, medicine, bibliography. Private premises.

H. P. KRAUS, 16 East 46th Street, New York, NY 10017. Telephone: (212) 687 4808. Incunabula, illuminated manuscripts, science.

D. and E. LAKE, 106 Berkeley Street, Toronto, Canada M5A 2W7. Telephone: (416) 863 9930. Americana, Canadiana, travel.

HARRY A. LEVINSON, Box 534, Beverly Hills, Ca. 90213. Telephone: (213) 276 9311. Early English books, fine printing. Private premises.

HOWARD S. MOTT, INC., South Main Street, Sheffield, Ma. 01257. Telephone: (413) 229 2019. English and American literature. Private premises.

KENNETH NEBENZAHL, INC., 333 North Michigan Avenue, Chicago, Il. 60601. Telephone: (312) 641 2711. Travel, Americana, atlases.

MAURICE F. NEVILLE, 835 Laguna Street, Santa Barbara, Ca. 93101. Telephone: (805) 963 1908. Modern American and English literature.

JEREMY NORMAN & CO., 442 Post Street, San Francisco, Ca. 94102. Telephone: (415) 718 6402. Medicine, science and technology.

B. and L. ROOTENBERG, PO Box 5049. Sherman Oaks, Ca. 91403. Telephone: (818) 788 7765. Science, medicine, history of ideas. Private premises.

JUSTIN G. SCHILLER LTD., 1 East 61st Street, New York, NY 10021. Telephone: (212) 832 8231. Children's books and illustrations, prints and drawings.

E. K. SCHREIBER, 135 East 65th Street, New York, NY 10021. Telephone: (212) 772 3150. Early and fine printing. Private premises.

C. A. STONEHILL, INC., 282 York Street, New Haven, Ct. 06511. Telephone: (203) 865 5141. English literature to the nineteenth century.

W. THOMAS TAYLOR, 708 Colorado, Austin, Tx. 78701. Telephone: (512) 478 7628. Fine and early printing, English and American literature, voyages.

LAURENCE WITTEN, PO Box 490, 181 Old Post Road, Southport, Ct. 06490. Telephone: (203) 255 3474. Early literature, incunabula, manuscripts. Private premises.

XIMENES RARE BOOKS, 19 East 69th Street, New York, NY 10021. Telephone: (212) 744 0226. English and American literature, manuscripts, science. Appointment preferable.

ZEITLIN & VER BRUGGE, 815 North La Cienega Boulevard, Los Angeles, Ca. 90069. Telephone: (213) 652 0784. Science and medicine, fine printing, general.

Continental Europe

THEODOR ACKERMANN, Ludwigstrasse 7, PO Box 23, 8000 München, West Germany. Fine arts, scholarly books, topography.

LIBRAIRIE PIERRE BERÈS, 14 Avenue de Friedland, 75008 Paris, France. Literature, fine printing and bindings.

BJÖRCK & BÖRJESSON, Strandvägen 7, PO Box 5404, 114 84 Stockholm, Sweden. Swedish literature, science, travel.

NICO ISRAEL, Keizersgracht 526, 1017 EK Amsterdam, Netherlands. Travel, atlases, science, natural history.

ANTIQUARIAAT JUNK BV, Van Eeghenstraat 129, 1017 GA Amsterdam, Netherlands. Natural history.

FRITZ NEIDHARDT, Relenbergstrasse 20, 7000 Stuttgart, West Germany. Illustrated books, natural history, prints.

LIBERERIA ANTIQUA PREGLIASCO, via Accademia Albertina 3 bis, 10123 Torino, Italy. Fine arts, topography, prints.

C. E. RAPPAPORT, Via Sistina 23, 00187 Roma, Italy. Early books, science, arts.

JÖRG SCHÄFER, Alfred-Escher-strasse 76, 8002 Zürich, Switzerland. Early books on theology (especially Reformation), prints, incunabula.

LIBRAIRIE THOMAS-SCHELER, 19 rue de Tournon, 75006 Paris, France. Early science and medicine, incunabula.

HELLMUT SCHUMANN, Rämistrasse 25, 8001 Zürich, Switzerland. Incunabula, illustrated books.

FL. TULKENS, rue du Chêne 21, 1000 Bruxelles, Belgium. Fine printing and bindings.

Australasia and South Africa

ARNOLD BOOKS, PO Box 22, Lincoln, Canterbury, New Zealand. Telephone: Christchurch 487643. Natural history, biological sciences. Private premises.

PETER ARNOLD, 463 High Street, Prahran, Victoria 3181, Australia. Telephone: (03) 529 2933. Australiana, Australian literature.

BERKELOUW, Bendooley, Hume Highway, Berrima, New South Wales 2577, Australia. Australiana, Pacific, anthropology.

CLARKE'S BOOKSHOP, 211 Long Street, Cape Town 8001, South Africa. Telephone: 235739. Africana, maps, travel.

STANLEY CLINGMAN, 206 Montrose, 36 Pritchard Street, Johannesburg, South Africa 2001. Telephone: 435589. Travel, Africana, natural history.

KENNETH HINCE, 138–40 Greville Street, Prahran, Victoria 3181, Australia. Australiana, literature, general.

TIM McCORMICK, 43 Queen Street, Woollahra, New South Wales 2025, Australia. Australiana.

JOHN SUMMERS BOOKSHOP, 224 Tuam Street, Christchurch, New Zealand. Telephone: Christchurch 798656. General.

NATIONAL ASSOCIATIONS

Almost all of the dealers listed above belong to their national associations: membership confers some respectability and also leads to participation in the fairs which the associations organize. Regular book fairs in Britain are organized by the Provincial Booksellers' Fairs Association (111 Park Road, New Barnet, Hertfordshire EN4 9QR): this is a good way for a new collector to meet dealers and see their stock without making the journey to each shop. The PBFA advertises its fairs in *Antiquarian Book Monthly Review*.

By writing to each association you can obtain a list of its members, divided by area so that you can find the nearest dealer specializing in your interest. Each association is a member of the International League of Antiquarian Booksellers (ILAB). The organizations in English-speaking countries are:

AUSTRALASIA Australian and New Zealand Association of Antiquarian Booksellers, PO Box 356, Prahran, Victoria 3181, Australia

CANADA Antiquarian Booksellers Association of Canada, 198 Queen Street West, Toronto, Ontario M5V 1Z2

UNITED KINGDOM Antiquarian Booksellers' Association, Book House, 45 East Hill, London SW18 2QZ

UNITED STATES OF AMERICA Antiquarian Booksellers Association of America, 50 Rockefeller Plaza, New York, NY 10020

Other national associations include:

BELGIUM Syndicat Belge de la Librairie Ancienne et Moderne, rue de Chêne 21, B–1000 Bruxelles

FRANCE Syndicat National de la Librairie Ancienne et Moderne, 47 rue Saint-André des Arts, F–75006 Paris

ITALY Associazione Librai Antiquari d'Italia, Via Jacopo Nardi 6, 50132 Firenze

SWITZERLAND Syndicat de la Librairie Ancienne et du Commerce de l'Estampe en Suisse, Schlossstrasse 6, FL–9490, Vaduz, Liechtenstein

WEST GERMANY Verband Deutscher Antiquare E.V., Unterer Anger 15, D–8000 München 2.

Further Reading

There are many books on the history of the book—there are even books about books about books—and many of them, even though published long ago and now out of print, are still used every day by collectors, librarians and booksellers. This short guide lists some of the standard works of reference, and includes those which are the most useful and approachable. But be warned: most of the best bibliographies, whether new or secondhand, are expensive, and a good reference library is costly to build.

Most good reference books will list the best works on their subjects. For a bibliography of an obscure subject or author, try T. Besterman, *A World Bibliography of Bibliographies* (Lausanne, fourth edition, 1965–6). For British authors, a similarly useful work is T. H. Howard-Hill, *Bibliography of British Literary Bibliographies* (Oxford, 1969). For dates in the history of printing, Colin Clair, *A Chronology of Printing* (London, 1969) is invaluable.

Be sure not to neglect the various journals. Both *The Library* (the quarterly journal of the Bibliographical Society of London) and the *Papers of the Bibliographical Society of America* (quarterly, New York) publish scholarly articles on all aspects of book production and printing history. More approachable are *The Book Collector* (quarterly, London) and *The American Book Collector* (every two months, New York), the former especially containing a wide range of significant articles. The best of the popular journals are *AB Bookman's Weekly* (weekly, Clifton, N.J.: really a trade journal but with some articles to entertain the collector) and *Antiquarian Book Monthly Review* (monthly, Oxford).

Finally, two important annual price guides deserve mention. *Book Auction Records* (Folkestone) and its American counterpart *American Book Prices Current* (New York) both index the year's auction results in Britain and America, and some European sales also, so that finding what a certain book last made at auction should be easy. *ABPC* also indexes manuscripts at auction, but *BAR* probably has the edge in accuracy. Beware, however, of using either book too glibly—the abbreviated nature of their entries sometimes makes it hard to tell why one copy of a book may have fetched twice its normal price. Avoid the *Lyle Official Books Review*, which can be misleading and inaccurate.

1. THE ART AND PRACTICE OF BOOK COLLECTING

Why Collect Books?

Good general guides to collecting include Alan G. Thomas, *Great Books and Book Collectors* (London, 1975) and Grant Uden, *Understanding Book Collecting* (London, 1982), while a number of interesting ideas are to be found in Jean Peters, ed., *Collectible Books: Some New Paths* (New York, 1979). Among the classic works in providing ideas are two by John Carter, *Taste and Technique in Book Collecting* (Cambridge, 1948) and *New Paths in Book Collecting* (London, 1934).

The Antiquarian Book Trade

Most of the books mentioned so far tell, by implication or definition, something of the history of the book trade, but there is no concise history (could there ever be such?) of the development of the art of printing and publishing. Studies of early printers include Martin Lowry, *The World of Aldus Manutius* (Oxford, 1979), Elizabeth Armstrong, *Robert Estienne, Royal Printer* (Cambridge, 1954) and Colin Clair, *Christopher Plantin* (London, 1960), while the stories of the finer printers of succeeding generations are usually better told through their bibliographies (some are cited below). Some notes on great English collectors and their libraries are to be found in Seymour de Ricci, *English Collectors of Books and Manuscripts 1530–1930* (Cambridge, 1930). The most comprehensive study of a single collector is probably A. N. L. Munby, *Phillipps Studies* (five parts, Cambridge, 1951–60); this was later reduced to a single more popular book, *Portrait of an Obsession* (London, 1967, edited by Nicolas Barker).

How to Read a Catalogue

The best further reading here is the catalogues themselves. The glossary on pp. 144–8 of this book will help with some of the terms, but the works by Peters, Carter and Hertzberger (cited there) are for all practical purposes comprehensive. A recent work on the history of book catalogues is Graham Pollard and John Ehrman, *The*

Distribution of Books by Catalogue (London, 1965), but this carries the story only as far as 1800.

Pitfalls

Almost all areas of book collecting have their traps for the uninitiated, and there are few books which deal specifically with this problem. Two rather specialized works will, however, be of interest: John Carter and Graham Pollard, *An Enquiry into the Nature of Certain Nineteenth-Century Pamphlets* (London, 1934, revised edition with a sequel by Nicolas Barker and John Collins, 1983) is as exciting as a detective story and should not be missed. William Voelkle, *The Spanish Forger* (New York, 1978), the catalogue of an exhibition at the Pierpont Morgan Library, describes all and illustrates most of the works then attributed to this ingenious deceiver.

2. TASTES AND TRENDS IN BOOK COLLECTING

In writing of the books dealing with a specific period or genre, distinction has to be drawn between comprehensive bibliographies, which simply attempt to list all known books on the subject, and discursive or digressive ones, which offer judgements as to the most valuable or useful. Discursive bibliographies are likely to be more approachable for the beginner, and some major bibliographical projects have not been included here. The reader should not assume that the following lists contain all the basic tools: they are meant only to introduce you to what is often a vast literature.

Early Printers and Fine Printing through the Ages

For incunabula the best one-volume reference work is F. R. Goff, *Incunabula in American Libraries* (New York, 1973), which indexes all known copies of fifteenth-century books in U.S. institutional libraries, together with some in private hands. Of general interest is Lotte Hellinga, *Caxton in Focus* (London, 1982).

Sixteenth-century books printed outside Britain are most efficiently listed in H. M. Adams, *Catalogue of Books Printed on the Continent of Europe 1501–1600 in Cambridge Libraries* (Cambridge, 1967: for English books of this period see following section). The studies of Robert Estienne and Christopher Plantin, both the founders of great printing dynasties, by Armstrong and Clair (referred to above) are particularly useful. A work of great distinction for all fine and early books is J. C. Brunet, *Manuel du libraire* (Paris, 1860).

Fine printing is an amorphous subject, but most of the great presses now have thorough bibliographies. The best are: Philip Gaskell, *The Foulis Press* (London, 1964) and the same author's *John Baskerville* (Cambridge, 1959; reprinted with additions, 1973); C. William Miller, *Benjamin Franklin's Philadelphia Printing* (Philadelphia, 1974); Allen T. Hazen, *A Bibliography of the Strawberry Hill Press* (New Haven, 1942); H. C. Brooks, *Compendiosa bibliografia di edizioni bodoniane* (Florence, 1927); Geoffrey Keynes,

William Pickering (London, 1924); William S. Peterson, *A Bibliography of the Kelmscott Press* (Oxford, 1984). There are also bibliographies of the Ashendene and Golden Cockerel Presses.

English Literature

Three comprehensive bibliogaphies aim to cover all English books to 1801: A. W. Pollard and G. R. Redgrave, *A Short-title Catalogue of English Books 1475–1640* (London, 1926; revised edition in progress, of which volume II was published in 1980); D. Wing, *A Short-title Catalogue . . . 1641–1700* (New York, 1945–51; revised edition in progress, of which volumes I–II were published in 1972 and 1982); and R. C. Alston and M. J. Crump, *The Eighteenth-century Short Title Catalogue: the British Library Collections* (London, 1983). These are known as STC, Wing and ESTC (BL) respectively. The last is only available on microfiche.

For English literary bibliographies, T. H. Howard-Hill, *A Bibliography of British Literary Bibliographies* (Oxford, 1969) will help you to find the best work. Many of the great figures in English literature have good descriptive bibliographies of their works, though there are a lot of surprising omissions and the progress of research in the past fifty years has made it difficult for any single scholar to distil it for publication. Standard works on great authors include those on Shakespeare (by William Jaggard, Stratford, 1911; and by Henrietta C. Bartlett, New Haven, 1922), Milton (K. A. Coleridge, Oxford, 1980); Pope (R. H. Griffith, Austin, Texas, 1922–7); Swift (H. Teerink and A. H. Scouten, Philadelphia, 1963); Johnson (W. P. Courtney and D. Nichol Smith, Oxford, 1925); Keats (J. R. MacGillivray, Toronto, 1949); Dickens (T. Hatton and A. H. Cleaver, London, 1933; and W. E. Smith, Los Angeles, 1981–2); Wilde (Stuart Mason, London, 1914); and Joyce (J. J. Slocum and H. Cahoon, New Haven and London, 1953).

Scientific and Medical Books

The most comprehensive collection of scientific books ever catalogued is that of Robert Honeyman, and the seven catalogues of *The Honeyman Collection* (London, Sotheby's, 1978–81) are an essential reference work. Honeyman's library included most of the classic works and some medical high spots (as well as hundreds of unsung books of importance such as the Connecticut telephone directory for 1878). Leslie T. Morton, *A Medical Bibliography* (London, fourth edition, 1983; known as 'Garrison and Morton') is the bible of medical collectors.

A quick reference guide for dates of early scientists and their publications is J. C. Poggendorff, *Biographisch-Literarisch Handwörterbuch zur Geschichte der exacten Wissenschaften* (Leipzig, 1863), while C. C. Gillespie, ed., *Dictionary of Scientific Biography* (New York, 1970–80) is a massive and excellent encyclopaedia of a more discursive kind, inevitably varying in quality but with bibliographies at the end of each entry.

Booksellers and collectors frequently use a number of

reference books which try to elect a pantheon of significant works. Among the most commonly cited are: Bern Dibner, *Heralds of Science* (Norwalk, Ct., and Washington, second edition, 1980), Harrison D. Horblit, *One Hundred Books Famous in Science* (New York, 1964: actually 130 titles, with collations but no commentary) and the influential *Printing and the Mind of Man* (London, 1967), edited by John Carter and P. H. Muir.

Americana and Australiana

The standard work for American imprints to 1800 is Charles Evans, *American Bibliography* (Chicago, 1903–34), while Jacob Blanck, *A Bibliography of American Literature* (New Haven, 1955–), still in progress, will eventually encompass the works of all significant American authors to 1930. A similarly ambitious work, Joseph Sabin, *A Dictionary of Books Relating to America* (New York, 1868–1936) covers travel, literature and imprints in its 29 volumes but is inevitably less comprehensive. Wright Howes, *U.S.-iana* (New York, 1962) is a selective guide to the most important books about the United States. The *Dictionary of American Biography* (New York, 1928–36, with later supplements) is an endlessly valuable work for its detail about obscure authors.

Australasia is also fortunate in its bibliographers. J. A. Ferguson, *Bibliography of Australia* (Sydney, 1941–69) lists all works on or printed in Australia from 1784 to 1900, and is based on the unrivalled collections at the Mitchell Library in Sydney and the National Library of Australia in Canberra. T. M. Hocken, *A Bibliography of Literature Relating to New Zealand* (Wellington, 1909) is similarly indispensable for the study of New Zealand books. The subject of Australasia is inextricably bound up with that of voyages of discovery, so works such as Hill (listed below) describe many other books which are of interest to the collector who limits himself to Australia and its neighbours.

Other bibliographies of early printing in developing countries include: Antonio Palau y Dulcet, *Manual del librero hispano-americano* (Barcelona, 1948–77) on Spain and Latin America; Sidney Mendelssohn, *South African Bibliography* (London, 1910) on the southern African states; and Rubens Borba de Moraes, *Bibliographia brasiliana* (Amsterdam, 1958) on Brazil.

Travel and Natural History Books

The most reliable bibliographies are often those which are based on a single collection, and in the field of English travel books the catalogues of the library of J. R. Abbey are supreme. These are: *Scenery of Great Britain and Ireland in Aquatint and Lithography 1770–1860* (London, 1952) and the companion volumes *Life in England* (London, 1953) and *Travel* (London, 1956–7), covering the same dates and media. Abbey's collection encompassed fine bindings and illuminated manuscripts (sold at auction in the 1960s and 1970s) but the collection of illustrated books was sold *en bloc* and is now in the Yale Center for British Art, New Haven. The catalogues are well illustrated with detailed descriptions often not found elsewhere. Illustrated books on all subjects are discussed and described in Sarah T. Prideaux, *Aquatint Engraving* (London, 1909: a pioneer study) and R. V. Tooley, *English Books with Coloured Plates* (Folkestone, 1978).

Further afield, travel in the Pacific is covered by Kenneth E. Hill, *The Hill Collection of Pacific Voyages* (San Diego, 1974–83) and the New South Wales Public Library *Bibliography of Captain James Cook* (Sydney, 1928). Most books on travel to America and other continents are found in the works which deal with that particular country's literature (see above).

Compared with travel books, there is a wealth of bibliographies of books on plants and animals. General studies on botanical books include Wilfrid Blunt and Sandra Raphael, *The Illustrated Herbal* (London, 1979), Wilfrid Blunt, *The Art of Botanical Illustration* (London, 1950) and Sacheverell Sitwell and Wilfrid Blunt, *Great Flower Books* (London, 1956). These are selective but informative. More technical and advanced are: *Catalogue of Botanical Books in the Collection of Rachel McMasters Miller Hunt* (Pittsburgh, 1958–61: a superbly produced and bibliographically immaculate book with useful notes), and Blanche Henrey, *British Botanical and Horticultural Literature before 1800* (Oxford, 1975: an exhaustive study of its subject).

Sacheverell Sitwell and others, *Great Bird Books* (London, 1953) is a lavish introduction to the subject, but the most important works for collectors of books on ornithology are the series by Claus Nissen, *Die illustrierte Vogelbücher* (Stuttgart, 1953), *Schöne Fischbücher* (Stuttgart, 1951) and *Die zoologische Buchillustration* (Stuttgart, 1966). These are dry bibliographies but essential for the serious collector.

The History of Ideas

This is a young subject and the bibliographies are few. The books listed in *Printing and the Mind of Man* (London, 1967, referred to above) serve as a selection on which the collector can concentrate his resources. This book has many drawbacks (notably its anglocentricity) but it is still invaluable as a guide to the field, and it lists many books not mentioned by standard bibliographies or works not previously thought of as collectable.

For economics, the standard works are the catalogues of the Kress Library of Business and Economics (Boston, 1940–67), of Luigi Einaudi (Turin, 1981) and the Goldsmiths' Library of Economic Literature at the University of London (Cambridge and London, 1970–83). See also R. D. Collison Black, *Catalogue of Pamphlets on Economic Subjects Published between 1750 and 1900 and now Housed in Irish Libraries* (Belfast, 1969), a useful work for the obscurer sort of publication. General histories of economic theory can also have their uses for collectors who are not experts on the subject. The best of these is probably the classic Joseph A. Schumpeter, *History of Economic Analysis* (London, 1954).

Often significant figures in politics and philosophy have been considered by bibliographers. Among these are Niccolò Machiavelli (bibliography by Adolph Gerber, Munich, 1912–13), Voltaire (Georges Bengesco, Paris, 1882–90), David Hume (T. E. Jessop, London, 1938) and Edmund Burke (William B. Todd, London, 1982). There are many others, to be found in Besterman's *World Bibliography of Bibliographies*, cited above.

Collecting Bindings

Binding history is an active subject. In Britain the pioneer has been the late Howard M. Nixon, whose books *Five Centuries of English Bookbinding* (London, 1978), *Sixteenth-century Gold-tooled Bindings in the Pierpont Morgan Library* (New York, 1971) and *English Restoration Bookbindings* (London, 1974) have identified many binders by their style and sets of tools. The catalogues of the Henry Davis Gift (London, 1979 and 1983), by Nixon's pupil and successor at the British Library, Mirjam M. Foot, incorporate many discoveries and will be a monument of binding history.

Because each binding is a separate artefact, it is impossible to compile reference works in the manner traditional with books. Reproductions, above all, are essential, and important information is to be found in illustrated auction catalogues such as those of J. R. Abbey (Sotheby's, London, 1966 and subsequent years) and booksellers' catalogues such as those of Maggs Bros. and Patrick King, both booksellers who specialize in bindings. The catalogue of the 1968 exhibition at the Bodleian Library, *Fine Bindings 1500–1700 from Oxford Libraries*, is particularly good and has summaries of binding styles.

Publishers' bindings of the nineteenth century are treated very differently, since by their nature they survive in more than one copy—though sometimes only a few examples can now be found. Ruari McLean, *Victorian Publishers' Book-bindings in Cloth and Leather* (London, 1974) is one of the best works on the subject, with many illustrations; it is complemented by the same author's *Victorian Publishers' Book-bindings in Paper* (London, 1983).

3. THE BOOK

The essential book for learning the basic rules of bibliography—and to remind yourself of the rules when you have forgotten them—is Philip Gaskell, *A New Introduction to Bibliography* (Oxford, 1972). This is fairly technical in places but it can help with understanding printing technology as well as bibliographical description. Colin Clair, *A Chronology of Printing* (London, 1969: referred to above) is helpful when you need to know odd facts such as when printing first reached Spain, or when Bodoni began work in Parma.

A short pamphlet published by the British Museum, *Looking at Prints*, gives a summary of the basic techniques for making prints and is equally applicable to book-illustration. Geoffrey Wakeman, *Victorian Book Illustration* (Newton Abbot, 1973) describes the platemaking processes in the nineteenth century, when a number of adventurous new methods were tried out. A. M. Hind, *The Processes and Schools of Engraving* (London, fourth edition, 1952) is good on technique although outdated as art history.

There is little published on conservation, though Bernard C. Middleton, *The Restoration of Leather Bindings* (Chicago, 1972; new edition, 1984) is good on the techniques employed by professional binders. A. D. Baynes-Cope, *Caring for Books and Documents* (London, British Museum, 1981) is brief but contains all the collector really needs to know.

Index

Numbers in italic refer to pages on which illustrations occur.

ACKNOWLEDGEMENTS

The majority of the illustrations in this book are reproduced from photographs from the archives of Christie's and Pickering & Chatto Ltd. Acknowledgement is also due to the following:

Reproduced by kind permission of the Marquess of Bath, 107(left)
Robin de Beaumont, 105
Reproduced by courtesy of the Board of the British Library, London, 103, 107(right), 110(left), 111
G. Bruckner ©, 19(left), 20(right)
City Art Centre, Edinburgh, 16
Reproduced by permission of the Henry E. Huntington Library, San Marino, California, frontispiece
By courtesy of the Library of Congress, Washington DC, 78, 101(left)
Mansell Collection, London, 13(right)
National Monuments Record, 9, 11(left)
National Portrait Gallery, London, 11(right)
Oxford University Press, 116(left)
Phillips Fine Art Auctioneers, New York, 42
Plantin-Moretus Museum, Antwerp, 117(top)
John Porter, 110(right)
By courtesy of Bernard Quaritch Ltd., 21, 24, 33(top), 68
St. Bride Printing Library, London, 114, 117(bottom), 118, 119, 120
By courtesy of Sotheby's, London, 57, 69, 71, 72, 89, 127(left)
Windsor Castle (Reproduced by gracious permission of Her Majesty the Queen), 18(left)
By courtesy of Zeitlin & Ver Brugge, Los Angeles, California, 20(left)

Our thanks are also due to Richard Miller, Alan Tabor and Dr Mirjam Foot; and to the Oxford University Press for permission to reproduce the drawing (p. 134) from P. Gaskell, *A New Introduction to Bibliography* (1972). The drawings on pp. 131, 132 and 133(bottom) are reprinted (in an amended form) by permission of the American Library Association from Bernard C. Middleton's *The Restoration of Leather Bindings*, Figs. 10, 34 and 44; copyright © 1972, 1984 (revised edition) the American Library Association.